MINNESOTA'S
MOST NOTORIOUS
MOBSTER

MINNESOTA'S **MOST NOTORIOUS** MOBSTER

The Making and Breaking of Kid Cann

RON DE BEAULIEU

THE History PRESS

Published by The History Press
Charleston, SC
www.historypress.com

First published 2025

Manufactured in the United States

ISBN 9781467158930

Library of Congress Control Number: 2024951899

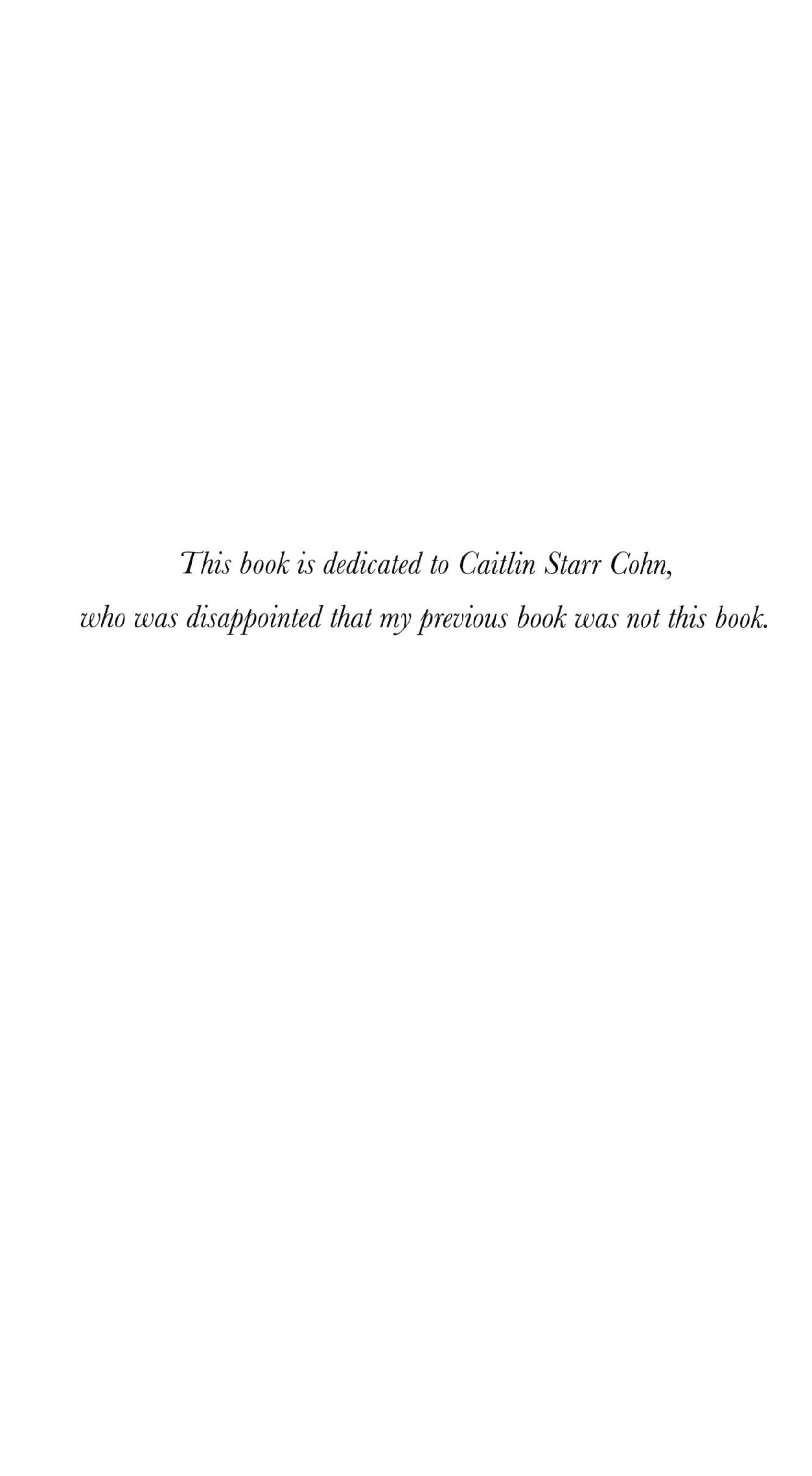

This book is dedicated to Caitlin Starr Cohn,

who was disappointed that my previous book was not this book.

CONTENTS

ACKNOWLEDGMENTS

Throughout the five years that I worked on this book, I received support and encouragement from more people than I can list here, and I appreciate all of it.

John Rodrigue, an editor at The History Press, read the first draft, and his critiques have made this version so much better. Artie Crisp, acquisitions editor, has been amazingly flexible, allowing me time to make improvements that probably matter to no one besides myself. Zoe Ames, concientious copyeditor, helped transform this from an informative but clumsy manuscript into a book worth reading.

Amy Lotsberg of the *Volsteadland* podcast reached out to me on social media and provided me with invaluable connections.

Dan Gray assisted me in reading through many primary sources for background information on early twentieth-century Minneapolis. Loren Hill not only shared with me more than seventy-two files of research he has gathered on the Minneapolis mob but also provided fact-checking and critiques for a draft of this book. Elizabeth Venditto, Scarlett O'Donovan and Chen-Yu Wu reviewed the resulting draft. In addition, Chen-Yu took some of the photographs, drove me to locations that were not easily accessible by public transportation and was effectively a single parent during the weeks when I spent every waking hour (and also some hours when I should have been sleeping) working on this book.

Friends and family members of Kid Cann and his associates gave me insights that I could not have gathered from archives. Not all of them want their names mentioned, but I can at least thank Sandra Brownstein for the stories she shared about her grandfather Abe "Brownie" Brownstein, a close friend of Kid Cann's.

Speaking of archives, the workers at the Gale Family Library at the Minnesota Historical Society Research Center and at the Hennepin County Library Special Collections assisted me over the course of about one hundred hours of research. An archivist at the National Archives of Chicago directed me to court records.

Michael Greenberg and Alex Weston, director/producer and artistic director, respectively, of *The Combination*, and crime novelist Christopher Valen helped me to understand how the legacy of Kid Cann fits into Minneapolitan cultural memory. Paul Maccabee, whom the St. Louis Park Historical Society rightfully considers the "Ultimate Kid Cann Historian," offered advice and answered questions as I worked my way to the end of this often perplexing project.

Calley did an excellent job keeping her brother Dino entertained while I worked; Dino did an excellent job playing with her.

INTRODUCTION

"Ninety percent of what was written about me is bullshit," mob boss Isadore "Kid Cann" Blumenfeld told reporters in 1976. Not that he was invested in setting the record straight—he had declined offers from professional authors willing to help write his autobiography. "I've got nothing to say really."[1]

The "facts" about his life, as written, are a jumble. A newspaper article published in his lifetime tells us, "Blumenfeld...grew up...on the Minneapolis northside where he was born Dec. 12, 1901."[2] None of that is true. Eric Wingard of the *Tribune* had known Kid Cann for six years when he wrote the article, and he may have been repeating (mis)information that his subject had given him. Information on file with the Board of Education Census Department indicates that his mother reported a 1900 birthdate for him.[3] But throughout his life, when Blumenfeld gave his age, he often provided a figure consistent with a December 1901 birthdate.

Even his name is something of a conundrum. Practically everyone in the written record spells Kid Cann's surname "Blumenfeld," but on his gravestone, it is spelled "Blumenfield."[4] Likewise, his death was recorded with Hennepin County under the name "Isadore Blumenfield," along with an incorrect place of birth.[5] On the witness stand as a defendant in a murder trial, Kid Cann testified that he used the last name "Bloom" because "Blumenfield is sort of a complicated name."[6] And that is only the tip of the iceberg. He used his brother's name, Harry Bloom, as an alias. He used his girlfriend's last name plus his brother's first name—Harry Lee—as an alias. He used apparently random names as aliases, their origins shrouded in mystery.

In this book, I will refer to him as "Isadore" because we know that name is *his*. As for why I don't just call him Kid Cann, well, it seemed unnecessarily hostile to write a book-length biography of a person while persistently referring to him by a nickname he eventually grew to hate. In fact, said Wingard, "the name 'Kid Cann' touches off an explosion [of anger] with him."[7]

That is but one difficulty involved in the process of compiling a biography of this man. He had an incentive to lie about himself in interviews with the press and with law enforcement and in his testimony in court. His associates also had an incentive to lie about him. This makes newspaper clippings, law enforcement "intelligence" and court testimony unreliable sources of objective data. Isadore would have lied (and he was known to have done so) for the sake of self-preservation, to stay out of trouble; his associates lied for the sake of self-preservation so that he would not hurt them. In addition, compulsive dishonesty is a job skill for career criminals, and mixing fantasy about themselves with reality was a feature of gangster culture in Isadore's era.[8] Local and state law enforcement were bound up with the mob—and not just with Isadore, who was one of many mobsters (I do not go into this in much detail in this book, but it was pervasive)—and for this reason, reports from these sources are suspect. Federal agencies, on the other hand, were too removed and betrayed, at times, cluelessness and credulity.

My goal with the narrative in this book is to make clear the origins of what we now believe about Isadore. This is not a full compendium of all things known or believed about Isadore—I tried to create one and went over the publisher's word limit. Making decisions about what to cut from a story is always difficult. I chose to prioritize page space for Isadore, and that meant taking out some information on his social environment. I've included the sources I used to write those excised sections in the bibliography, for further reading. In addition, I have left out incidents in which Isadore was questioned by law enforcement regarding crimes that were committed by other people and that do not appear to have otherwise involved him, unless they are necessary for background.

Isadore has become a figure of local folklore, about whom much has been said and much has been written—much of it false. But there is more to folklore than objective truth and falsehood. The epilogue discusses the legacy of folkloric beliefs through portrayals of Isadore in fiction, communicating truth beyond the verifiable about the man who was "the closest thing Minnesota had to a godfather."[9]

Chapter 1

UNHEALTHY INFLUENCE

"Clean and Sweet"

"It is amazing that a large, intelligent community like Minneapolis could be visited for so long by the unhealthy criminal influence of an Isadore Blumenfeld and company," groused Judge Edward Devitt in 1961. He said it without a trace of irony.[10]

The rot of municipal corruption ran deep in Minneapolis. Mayor Albert Alonzo "Doc" Ames's ill-fated fourth term began in January 1901, when Isadore was still a baby.[11] When Ames was in office, he "unleashed a race for loot at dizzying speed....The boundaries between the mayor, the police and the lowest of hoodlums evaporated."[12] As Ames biographer Erik Rivenes notes, this was Ames's fourth term as mayor, and each term had been tainted, going back to 1877. By the time Minneapolitans elected him yet again in 1900, they knew the kind of mayor he was going to be.

In the wake of the Ames scandal, which resulted in a wave of high-profile trials, Alderman D. Percy Jones, president of the Minneapolis City Council, was appointed acting mayor. Once in that position, Jones worked to untangle the knots tying the mayor's office and the police department to the vice trades. In conversation with author Lincoln Steffens, Jones admitted that this might not be a realistic approach. "Can a city be governed without any alliance with crime? It was an open question." But "Minneapolis should be clean and sweet for a little while at least, and the new administration should begin with a clear deck."[13]

The cartoonist at the *Minneapolis Tribune* seemed confident that the Hennepin County Grand Jury would keep Minneapolis corruption at bay in May 1901. *Courtesy of Hennepin County Library.*

For all Jones's efforts, the Minneapolis into which Phillip and Eva Blumenfield brought their toddler son, Isadore, retained elements of corruption. Not that the place the Blumenfields came from was healthier for them. Phillip, a cabinetmaker, hailed from Russia, but he and Eva had started their family in Râmnicu Sărat, Romania. It was there that Isadore, their first child, was born on September 8, 1900. Fifteen years earlier, in 1875, following a series of bloody pogroms (organized, coordinated campaigns of rape, pillage and murder conducted against Jewish communities) the premier

Dr. Albert A. Ames, 1900. *Courtesy of Hennepin County Library.*

of Romania decided to enforce long-ignored anti-Jewish laws: Jews were no longer allowed to live in the countryside, yet those who dwelt in cities were labeled vagrants, a status that permitted their expulsion from the country.

Mr. and Mrs. Blumenfield and their little boy made their first landing in North America in Canada. From there, they took the SS *Lakeboat* to Duluth and then made their way to Minneapolis, where they lived at 824 Seventh Street South.

When the Blumenfields came to the south side of Minneapolis, they joined a preexisting community of Romanian Jews. There were very few areas of the city where Jews could find housing: Seward, Cedar-Riverside and the Northside area now known as Near North. Real estate values were lower in these neighborhoods. Many Gentile landlords refused to rent to Jews, writing a "Gentiles only" requirement into their rental notices.[14]

The rabbi Dr. Maurice H. Lefkovits, who came to Minneapolis after World War I, wrote in 1922, "Minneapolis Jewry enjoys the painful distinction of being the lowest esteemed community in the land so far as the non-Jewish population of the city is concerned."[15] Anti-Jewish employment discrimination was a particular hurdle in Minneapolis, with job ads specifying "Gentile" or "Gentiles Preferred," and employers believed in Jewish stereotypes that made them think Jews would be difficult employees. Young Minneapolitan Jews took various paths to escape poverty. Some, like Augie Ratner, Benny Haskell and Ernie Fliegel, pursued athletics and became professional boxers. A friend of Isadore's from his youth said that "he took the name Kid Cann when he wanted to be a boxer," although Isadore didn't go into that professionally.[16]

Other young Jewish men focused on attaining higher education and the ticket to white-collar professions it provided.[17] But even so, the most respected of occupations offered no sure path to success, thanks to workplace discrimination against Jewish physicians and the difficulty Jewish attorneys faced in attracting clients.[18] This path was foreclosed to Isadore by his lack of academic gifts. In his early sixties, he would describe his level of education as "third grade" and assert "that he can read to a very limited extent and that he often encounters words which he cannot understand."[19] On paper,

Above: Interior of Minneapolis City Hall, *Father of Waters* statue, 1907. *Courtesy of Hennepin County Library.*

Opposite: Looking north on First Avenue North from Sixth Street, 1907. *Courtesy of Hennepin County Library.*

Isadore was enrolled as a student in Minneapolis public schools from 1906 to 1915, but in fact, he stopped attending class at age eleven to work full time as a newsboy. Even before that, he was putting bread on the table—literally.[20] According to a news story published in his adulthood:

> *When Blumenfeld was a boy, wholesale bakers used to deliver their loaded bread-boxes at the front or side doors of grocery stores during the wee hours of the morning.*
>
> *Young Isadore would surreptitiously leave a warm bed in the early a.m. to beat the grocer to the box so the Blumenfeld family could eat.*[21]

That family grew to eight people, with two more boys—Harry, born in 1908, and Isaac "Yiddy" (both of whom legally shortened their last name to "Bloom"), born in 1911—and three girls: Ann, born in 1905; Ethel, born

in 1906; and Mary, born in 1912. There was nothing unusual about a child of Isadore's generation contributing income, but the depth of the struggles of Isadore's family was exceptional. Their sickly father was in and out of Hennepin County Tuberculosis Sanitarium.[22] When he was out, he worked, and the year of Yiddy's birth, Phillip was listed in the Minneapolis phone directory as a peddler. In 1915 and 1916, he did various kinds of repair

Above: Minnehaha Falls, 1907. *Courtesy of Hennepin County Library.*

Opposite: Augie Ratner, 1920. *Courtesy of Hennepin County Library.*

work; in 1918, he and Isadore were both listed as peddlers. This was the occupation Phillip would hold for the next few years, leading up to his untimely death.[23] He was not the only invalid in the family. When Ann was nine years old, she, too, developed tuberculosis.

The family moved repeatedly during Isadore's childhood. Later, he would not precisely recall the street addresses or locations of the family's residences or how long they lived in each. There were too many, and he had been too young and, probably, overwhelmed. When he was still a little boy, the family moved to Fourth Street and, later, to 1515 Fifth Street South. The year after Yiddy was born, and the same year in which Mary was born, they lived at 421 Sixteenth Avenue South. Isadore remembered the family next living on Elliot Avenue between Nineteenth and Twentieth Streets. When Isadore was about fourteen or fifteen years old, "I was big enough to be on my own," he recalled. "I still stayed at home, but I was away two or three days at a time and would come back."[24]

According to Yiddy, the monthly rent at the Fourth Street address was $2.25 (about $32 in today's dollars), and one reason for the family's moves was that "the children became older and were able to give more financial help at home…so the family's rental quarters gradually improved." In the years after Isadore started spending less time at home, the family moved again and again and again. To get free fuel for the family home, Yiddy walked along the railroad tracks to pick up coal to sell. He, too, worked as a newsboy.[25]

"Newsboy" sounds like a cute job title, but it was rough work, scrambling with other children for a street corner on Newspaper Row. One unkind theory about how Isadore got his nickname held that he shied away from violence and hid in the latrine (the "can") when fights broke out. The newsboys also had trouble with their employers, and when Isadore was an older teenager, they organized a strike. Governor Burnquist sent out the National Guard against them.[26]

In Minnesota, the early twentieth century was an era of "scandal sheets," which exposed all and sundry, including the children who sold them, to salacious tales of sex and corruption. In 1914, the scandal sheet editor Howard Guilford moved from St. Paul to Minneapolis. He allowed himself to be pulled into an established system of political graft. In his own defense, he said, referring to a time that he committed extortion, "It was everybody's and nobody's boodle....One hundred and one per cent of the genus homo would practice it if they had the chance."[27]

Above: Businesses on Newspaper Row, 1914. *Courtesy of Hennepin County Library.*

Opposite, top left: Roy N. Miner, "exalted cyclops of the Minneapolis chapter of the Ku Klux Klan," 1923. Endemic antisemitism in Minneapolis allowed the KKK to find a home there. *Courtesy of Hennepin County Library.*

Opposite, top right: Benny Haskell, 1920. *Courtesy of Hennepin County Library.*

Opposite, bottom: Minneapolis City Hall soon after completion, 1906. *Courtesy of Hennepin County Library.*

Left: Arthur Rowe, proprietor of the Elroy Hotel, on trial in a case involving bribery for police protection, 1916. *Courtesy of Hennepin County Library.*

Right: Orren M. Wassing, private secretary to Mayor Thomas Van Lear, 1916. Wassing was convicted of rape after he paid the parents of a teenager to allow him to sleep with their daughter. *Courtesy of Hennepin County Library.*

Guilford was an editor of the *Twin City Reporter*, a mean-spirited, bigoted rag, in addition to being a pretext for extortion. Ed Morgan, a gambling racketeer who was one of the most—if not *the* most—powerful underworld figures in Minneapolis, ran the paper, sometimes with Guilford and sometimes with Jack Bevans, who was a pimp as well as a journalist.

On January 1, 1917, Guilford left the *Reporter.* "No matter what was contained in the headlines and columns of the paper, the news boys insisted on shouting out, [about prostitution]." He blamed the children for their sales tactic: "The newsies knew that the very nicest people, particularly the dear ladies, just loved to read sex scandal so they could shock themselves, and the cry helped to sell papers."[28]

By that time, Isadore was sixteen years old and had found more ways of making an income, none of them sufficing to raise his family out of poverty. He would never forget his humble origins, no matter how far he grew from the urchin he had been. A woman who became friends with Isadore when he was in his fifties remembered, "[Isadore] would tell us stories about his poor background as a Rumanian immigrant." In addition to newspaper sales, he busied himself with "picking up bus transfers that people had dropped and reselling them for pennies....He'd bring coffee to the downtown whorehouses for the tips."[29] These efforts were typical of his social class and generation, as well as the one before and the one to follow, and should not be taken as evidence of predisposition to a life of crime.[30] At some point in his teenage years, he did become a pimp, which would have involved him in a longstanding criminal network that relied on bribery of police officials.

THE SETTLER-COLONISTS OF EARLY Minneapolis, some of whom were still alive during Isadore's childhood, were for the most part White, Anglo-Saxon Protestants from New England who had established the city's major industries and "set the tone of exclusivity and discrimination that was perpetuated by other non-Jewish residents."[31]

Hennepin County Pioneers Celebration at the Exposition Building, sometime around the turn of the twentieth century (between 1896 and 1907). *Courtesy of Hennepin County Library.*

Radisson Hotel, 1908. *Courtesy of Hennepin County Library.*

The high society that ruled Minneapolis during Isadore's childhood threw lavish receptions and balls in celebration of itself, dolled up in absurd finery.[32] In 1909, there was a ball at the Radisson Hotel. Isadore would likely not have known about it. He also would not have known that one day, he would host parties at the Radisson.

City leaders were aware that poverty was a problem, but they seem to have concerned themselves more with the aesthetics of poverty than with

Gateway Park, 1915. *Courtesy of Hennepin County Library.*

Crowd gathered at Gateway Park dedication, 1915. *Courtesy of Hennepin County Library.*

Adath Jeshurun Synagogue, 3200 Dupont Avenue South, 1927. *Courtesy of Hennepin County Library.*

Beth El Jeshurun Synagogue, 1349 Penn Avenue North, 1926. *Courtesy of Hennepin County Library.*

the plight of impoverished people. "Topping the to-do list of [reformers] was removal of what many referred to as 'urban blight.'...Critics worried about the [unsightly and unsafe condition of buildings] and about the... inhabitants themselves (often lumped misleadingly into a single 'floating population' of transients)." Rather than provide funding to help residents or their landlords improve the conditions of the buildings, "Minneapolis... demolished about four blocks of the Bridge Square district, including the old City Hall, to make way for a new neighborhood called the Gateway. Its centerpiece was a grand pavilion surrounded by a lovely public park," which opened to great fanfare in 1915. In a darkly humorous twist, the "transients" who had lost their homes now hung around the beautiful new park, as did "respectable" people, who had to cross paths with living reminders of municipal cruelty and failure.[33]

No help could be expected from city leadership. Settlement houses provided social services, and religious organizations, among them synagogues, went to great lengths to help stabilize low-income communities, but it was never enough.[34] And those who suffered most from the bite of poverty and indifference in early twentieth-century Minneapolis were the Jews, whose community had grown in numbers but not in power.[35]

The lucrative opportunities that Prohibition soon offered proved enticing, and Isadore succumbed to the unhealthy influence of Minneapolis.

Juvenile Delinquent

Isadore was first arrested on May 22, 1920, a few months before his twentieth birthday. Back then, twenty-one was the age of majority, and he was still legally a minor child. That does not seem to have figured into his treatment by the authorities. He was charged with being "found in a disorderly house," a term that colloquially meant "brothel," but under Minnesota statutes, it could also have been any place in which "the peace, comfort, or decency of a neighborhood is habitually disturbed."[36] Isadore was fined five dollars (about seventy-eight dollars in today's currency), a sizable sum for a teenager.

Frank A. Regan, Minneapolis Police Department chief of detectives, 1915. *Courtesy of Hennepin County Library.*

Three weeks later, on June 11, he was arrested again, this time for picking pockets. Described by the police as a "Roumanian carnival man" aged twenty-two (meaning that he lied to them about his age), Isadore had been "working crowds at a Norwegian church gathering at the Armory." He was subjected to bertillonage, an extensive system of measurement of criminals designed to aid in identification. A French police clerk, Alphonse Bertillon, invented it in 1883, and it was already considered obsolete in 1920, fingerprinting having overtaken it. The Minneapolis Police Department was behind the times. And so,

> *Officer Jones set to work, measuring eleven other parts of Blumenfeld's body. Jones calculated the height and length of his head; the length of his left, middle and little fingers; his left foot; his left forearm; his right ear; his outstretched arms; and finally his trunk (the distance from the top of the head to a bench, for a seated person). He noted that Blumenfeld had a full set of teeth.*[37]

His height was recorded as five feet, five inches and his weight as 142 pounds. The logbook of the Bureau of Identification within the Minneapolis Police Department states that he was examined the day after his arrest and that he received an unspecified sentence. His police record says only that Captain Regan released him on June 12.[38]

Such low-level, nonviolent offenses still did not predict the career that was to follow for Isadore.

Chapter 2

THE TWENTIES ROAR

Getting Started

The Eighteenth Amendment was ratified by the states on January 16, 1919, and slated to take effect one year later, at which time "the manufacture, sale, or transportation of intoxicating liquors within, the importation thereof into, or the exportation thereof from the United States and all territory subject to the jurisdiction thereof for beverage purposes is hereby prohibited."[39]

Notably, the amendment "banned but did not define 'intoxicating liquors,'" and as a result, some congressmen voted for it "assum[ing] that it referred to liquor and would exempt beer and wine." The leader of the Anti-Saloon League had different ideas when he drafted the National Prohibition Act, which Minnesota representative Andrew Volstead, chairman of the House Judiciary Committee, sponsored. The Volstead Act, as it came to be called, "defined an intoxicating beverage as anything that contained more than *one half of one percent* alcohol" (emphasis mine). President Woodrow Wilson vetoed it; the House and the Senate overrode his vote on October 28, 1919. "The result was a decade of lawlessness, with citizens flouting the law at speakeasies and bootleggers corrupting public officials."[40]

Congress had added a religious exemption to the Prohibition Act: the purchase and consumption of wine would be permitted for "sacramental purposes." This meant that Jews and some sects of Christianity, including

Catholics, could legitimately access alcohol for their religious services. These religious communities thus had some advantage in the new shadow economy of Prohibition-era America.

A.J. Volstead. *Library of Congress Prints and Photographs Division.*

Foreseeing this and fearing the implications for how they would be perceived by Gentiles, some Jewish leaders looked askance at the exemption. They were leery of special laws for Jews after harrowing experiences with legal policies that singled out Jews back in Europe.[41] But Prohibition would usher in an era of law-scoffing that would spread to Jews and Gentiles alike. The tough-guy gangster persona that Isadore and company embraced was culturally normative for American males of their generation.[42]

Throughout the United States, the Ku Klux Klan used the inevitable and immediately apparent failure of Prohibition's aims as an excuse to carry out its own vigilante oppression. There was a subculture of "Prohibition-supporting white Protestants who thought that the law wasn't doing enough to stop the bootleggers they read about in the tabloids," and the KKK "sold itself to those people as a law enforcement organization." Its focus in this period was on European immigrants. Klan membership grew between 1920 and 1925, at which point the organization boasted an official count in the millions.[43] It was active in Minnesota and had a chapter in Minneapolis, where prejudice against Jews soared. "Local activity of Jewish hoodlums and gangsters in the 1920s…contributed to Minneapolitans' low opinion of Jews," writes historian Laura Weber.[44] Isadore was among those hoodlums, and as his notoriety increased over the decades to come, he became an excuse for antisemites to maintain their prejudices against the Jewish community, even as Gentile gangsters operated right alongside him.[45]

On the morning of January 20, 1923, an armed robbery at the Payne Avenue State Bank in St. Paul ended with a dead cop and a dying cashier.[46] Police officers raided the Minneapolis home of a man involved in the robbery, where they arrested two men, one of whom gave his name as "Harry Bloom." It was twenty-two-year-old Isadore who often gave Harry's name as a pseudonym. Isadore was held in jail for some days, but then he was released for good.

Near Beer Saloon on 1301 Marshall Street NE, 1919. Near beer, a malt beverage with less than 0.5 percent ABV, would continue to be legal under national Prohibition. *Courtesy of Hennepin County Library.*

There was no evidence linking Isadore to the bank robbery, but the promise of the big payday it could have yielded must have been tempting to him at the time. When his father died later that year, on June 16, the family had to borrow ten dollars for a pine box to bury him in, Isadore said later.[47] After Phillip's death, Isadore "assumed the support of the family and coached his

Nicollet Avenue looking north from Eighth Street, 1920. *Courtesy of Hennepin County Library.*

Looking north on Hennepin Avenue from Washington Avenue, 1923. *Courtesy of Hennepin County Library.*

Nicollet Avenue from Third Street to Fourth Street, looking south, sometime in the 1920s. *Courtesy of Hennepin County Library.*

brothers on what they should do" to join him in bootlegging.[48] It was a good time for it. That same year, the Clay County attorney wrote to Assistant Attorney General Willebrandt, "The [liquor supply] at Minneapolis seems to be without limit."[49]

Despite the great responsibility that had been foisted on him by his father's death, Isadore was still a young man, only twenty-three years old on April 19, 1924, and he acted with youthful impetuousness when he got into a 3:00 a.m. fight with his friend Abe Percansky over a girl.

> *As the police have pieced the story together, Percansky and Bloom* [referring to Isadore] *became engaged in an altercation in front of the* [Vienna Café at 322 Nicollet Avenue in Minneapolis], *blows were exchanged, and Percansky drew a gun which Bloom took away from him, according to the story of other witnesses....Bloom gave the gun back to Percansky and words were passed which resulted in another fist fight, the witnesses said.*

> *At this point* [Charles] *Goldberg, endeavoring to act as a mediator, stepped into the fray to separate the fighters. A shot rang out and Goldberg fell to the sidewalk.*

Such was the understanding at that time, suggesting that Percansky shot Goldberg. Three days later, the *Minneapolis Star Journal* reported that the Hennepin County attorney had issued a complaint for assault against Percansky, who remained incarcerated. Percansky's lawyer, Archibald M. "Archie" Cary, requested an examination, and bail was set at $10,000.

Goldberg died from his injury. And yet Percansky did not go to trial. Isadore confessed, explaining that it had been an accident. The Hennepin County Grand Jury deliberated on the case and declined to indict him. Isadore would face no trial, no consequences; neither would Percansky.

A few months after Goldberg's death, a sheriff's deputy in Illinois arrested Abe Percansky and a woman who were speeding on the highway. Their Packard, which had a Minnesota license plate, held 119 gallons of pure grain alcohol. The authorities "figured he was part of a smuggling ring between Chicago and Minneapolis. They were right."[50]

As for Isadore, he also did not always get away with bootlegging scot-free, but he came close. On September 24, 1927, he was charged in federal court in Minneapolis with violating the National Prohibition Act. He and his codefendant, John Sisson, faced a charge of "nuisance," and Isadore also had a charge of "possession [of bootlegged alcohol]" lodged against him. Five days after he was charged, the prosecution filed a nolle prosequi (declining to pursue the case, also referred to as "nolling") on the nuisance count; as for possession, Isadore paid a $400 fine on November 1.[51] In today's dollars, that's $7,219.98.

In a few months' time, Isadore would face a graver charge than bootlegging.

Shoot-Out at the Cotton Club

The Cotton Club, located at 718 Sixth Avenue North in Minneapolis, was one of many so-called black-and-tan establishments on that street. Black and tans catered to patrons of all races despite the era's typical racial segregation. Like many of its neighbors, the Cotton Club provided gambling, entertainment and bootleg liquor.[52] "For many years," writes Jay Goetting, a jazz bass player and journalist, "Minneapolis's Near Northside was a most-happening locale for clubs....Beginning during Prohibition, musicians played on Hennepin Avenue six or seven nights per week."[53]

It was a heady time and place, and the Cotton Club was typical. Owned by the Black restaurateur William Pugh, the club was a "chicken shack" that provided its customers with good food "and dancing and fighting all night....Hungry men went [there] to feast on legs and breasts," snarks twenty-first century writer Brian P. Rubin, "served on plates as well as in cocktail dresses."[54]

In the early morning on Friday, February 3, 1928, violence broke out at the club, under circumstances that will be forever shrouded in confusion. "The joint was jumping" that night. A bootlegger and former sheriff, Verne Miller, danced with Valencia "Shuffle Along" Nay, who was employed as an "entertainer." Accounts of what happened immediately after that varied. Another patron, Jack Sackter, who described Nay as a "friend," spoke to her, and Isadore "told Sackter to leave her alone." Then, unprovoked, Miller pistol-whipped Sackter. The other version of the story is that Sackter was verbally disrespectful to Nay, and that was why Miller hit him.[55]

Other patrons surrounded these men and settled them down, while a witness called the police "and informed them a pistol had been drawn at the [club]."[56] It does not appear that an officer was dispatched to the scene.

Jack Sackter left in a taxi. He saw two patrolmen, James H. Trepanier and Bernard Wynne, and reported the assault to them. Trepanier was a relative outsider to this part of town, as he lived at 4214 Nicollet Avenue South with his wife and two young daughters. He was a veteran of World War I who had joined the Minneapolis Police Department in his late twenties and was now thirty-two years old. Before his transfer to the North Side patrol, he had been a motorcycle cop and had earned a citation for bravery in 1924 for the capture of a bandit.

Wynne was patrolling closer to his home at 3823 Bryant Avenue North, but he had been around the block in more ways than one. The thirty-nine-year-old policeman, also a World War I veteran, had taken three bullets in his legs. That had happened here, in Minneapolis, in 1926. Wynne's partner had been shot to death.[57]

After their conversation with Sackter, Trepanier and Wynne proceeded to the Cotton Club to investigate the assault. They arrived at five o'clock in the morning and knocked on the door. Isadore "opened it a crack." He told the policemen, "The trouble's over. We're closing up."[58] The cops drew their guns and shoved the door open in spite of him.[59] Trepanier went ahead into the club to find a few people still there. One news account put the number at six men; Trepanier remembered it as about a dozen; in the account accepted by the MPD Federation, the number of patrons was more than twice that high. Trepanier told all present to put up their hands.[60] According to one version of events, Trepanier and Wynne began to search the men and found two guns left on chairs. The policemen "believed they had all the men disarmed....Wynne [had] stepped to a telephone in another room to summon a patrol wagon when the shooting began."[61]

In another version, Trepanier said to his partner, "Call the [patrol] wagon while I search them."[62] Wynne walked over to the telephone, and Trepanier approached the first person in line. At that moment, on the other side of the room, someone overturned a table. Five men took up places behind it. The outnumbered police officers glared at them. The five men glared back. In a "sudden movement," one of those men drew his pistol and fired it in the direction of Trepanier and Wynne. Immediately, several men who had been waiting in line to be searched drew pistols as well.[63]

Trepanier later testified that the "shooting opened...as Harry Bloom, alias 'Kid' Cann, started to move toward the rear door."[64] Trepanier was shot twice in the abdomen, and he fell. Wynne took a bullet to the leg. He staggered. According to one account, he stayed upright.[65] According to another, he fell.[66] Although wounded, said a news report, "both officers opened fire, and Bloom, crouching behind a chair, was hit in the thigh."[67] This understates the chaos. Trepanier was under the impression that Miller had shot him, and, he said, "I began shooting in the direction of Miller.... My partner...was between me and the front door, and he began shooting. [Then] the firing became quite general."[68]

The version provided on the MPD Federation website is straight out of an action movie.

> *Both patrolmen returned the fire. For a moment Pandemonium reigned. Pistols barked and filled the small hall with their roar. Bullets thudded into the walls, splintered chairs and tables and broke out windows. Women and men alike screamed, dodging, scurrying and fighting to cover. Patrons turned over tables and cowered behind them, fear in their eyes.*
>
> *Officer Trepanier, stretched on the floor, groaning from his wounds, braced his right arm with his left hand and emptied his pistol at armed men in the place.*
>
> *Officer Wynne...* [also] *emptied his pistol at the crowd and, despite the pain of his wound, brought them to order. Waving his...pistol at the disordered mob, he commanded, "Now all of you line up and be quiet."*[69]

Officer Trepanier, shooting victim, 1928. *Courtesy of Hennepin County Library.*

Wynne finally called MPD HQ, and a gun squad arrived. Wynne identified Isadore as the shooter. When Isadore's gun was examined, it was found to have three empty clips. Under guard, Isadore was brought to General Hospital. He gave his name to police as Harry Bloom. As for Verne Miller, he had escaped the club through the back door during the shootout.

Trepanier lay in serious condition at General. He had received two blood transfusions. Wynne was released within twelve hours. Isadore was taken to jail after getting his wound treated. His condition deteriorated, and he was brought back to the hospital.

The Hennepin County Grand Jury indicted Isadore, Miller and two other men—a Sioux Falls, South Dakota fight manager and a barkeeper from St. Paul—on charges of first degree assault. Miller was on the lam. Isadore was out of the hospital and well enough to go to court on February 16, where he pleaded not guilty and posted a $2,500 bond.

In November, the county attorney's office filed a nolle prosequi regarding all four defendants in the Cotton Club shooting, "for the reason that the State lacked sufficient evidence to sustain a verdict of guilty."[70] The reason was "a failure of witnesses"—even though Trepanier gave testimony that Verne Miller was the shooter.[71]

Trepanier retired from the force. He was paralyzed from the waist down. He spent the next ten years in and out of the hospital to deal with the long-term symptoms of his injury. He turned to jewelry making and watch repair and opened a shop at Lake Street and Chicago Avenue South. It did not last, owing to his hospital stays. Determined to support his family, he brought a jewelry repair bench to the hospital and worked whenever he was strong enough to sit up.

For ten years, Trepanier fought for his health, but on September 20, 1938, he died at the age of forty-two, survived by his wife and daughters. He lived longer than Verne Miller, whose judgment was badly affected by untreated syphilis.[72] After a riotous five years of murder and mayhem that brought him into contact and partnership with a rogue's gallery of public enemies, Miller had the dubious distinction of seeing his name on the FBI's Most Wanted list. In late autumn of 1933, "Verne Miller's nude, trussed-up, and beaten body [was] found on the outskirts of Detroit....The corpse was wrapped in a cheap Saxton auto robe."[73]

A newspaper would incorrectly report, many years later, that Isadore "was indicted for the killing of two Minneapolis police officers at the Cotton Club, which indictment was dismissed for lack of evidence" and the FBI would repeat this in its files.[74] Isadore remains (mis)remembered to this day as a double-homicide cop killer.[75]

Men of Their Time

Astute observers foresaw the bootlegging bonanza that Prohibition would bring. They planned accordingly. Thanks to a ban on importation of whiskey during World War I, illicit strategies for bringing liquor into the country were already well known to interested parties. Minnesota's Commission for Public Safety had imposed wartime anti-vice policies that ended up functioning, against the intentions of the commissioners, as a dress rehearsal for national Prohibition.

In December 1919, what later came to be called the Winnipeg Liquor Conspiracy took shape: seventy-four barrels of whiskey were to be placed in gondola railcars that were mostly filled with scrap metal and then smuggled from Winnipeg down to a Minneapolis scrapyard. Saul Goldberg, a co-conspirator, approached Mike Weisman, a Minneapolis pimp, asking him to handle things with the local authorities so that they would not interfere with the operation.

Howard Guilford, according his memoir, worked with Archie Cary to investigate the plot. The conspirators included both Hennepin County Attorney William M. "Bud" Nash and Sheriff Oscar Martinson, the former Minneapolis chief of police. It came out in due course that Nash had also protected his brother John, a brothel owner, from prosecution.[76] Bud Nash's subsequent removal from office paved the way for Assistant Hennepin County Attorney Floyd Bjørnstjerne Olson.

Olson, born in 1891 to immigrant parents (a Norwegian father and a Swedish mother), had a slightly more privileged upbringing than most of his neighbors on the North Side. His playmates preferred to come over to his house because his mother, Ida, gave them treats. Floyd's father, Paul, had a steady but low-status manual labor job, and Ida constantly harangued him about his lack of ambition. Floyd hated the tension between them and preferred to go to his friends' houses—especially Abe Harris's.[77]

The Harris family was Jewish, as were almost all the children in Floyd's friend group. He learned to speak fluent Yiddish and served as a Shabbos goy, a Gentile who carries out tasks on the Sabbath that Jews are restricted by religious law from doing themselves. When entering a synagogue, Olson knew to cover his head with a yarmulke. As a candidate for Hennepin County attorney and, later, governor of Minnesota, he would come back to the North Side, speaking Yiddish at campaign events and while casually chatting with elders. After Olson's death, one of his colleagues would write in a touching tribute to the late governor that, on long road trips across the state

Opposite: Floyd B. Olson and his daughter, 1924. *Courtesy of Hennepin County Library.*

Above, left: Oscar Martinson, Hennepin County sheriff, participated in a whiskey-smuggling plot with Nash, 1920. *Courtesy of Hennepin County Library.*

Above, right: Hennepin County Attorney William M. "Bud" Nash was a co-conspirator in a whiskey-smuggling plot. *Courtesy of Hennepin County Library.*

of Minnesota, Olson would break out in song. He could sing in multiple Scandinavian languages—and Yiddish.[78]

"Governor Floyd B. Olson…was known to bend elbows with a number of local gangsters, including Kid Cann, the most notorious mobster Minnesota would ever produce. The two had actually grown up in the same Minneapolis neighborhood," reads a 2007 article on a Minnesota news site.[79] That second sentence, though reflective of a popular local belief, is untrue. Olson was ten years Isadore's senior, and the latter was brought up in South Minneapolis. By the time Isadore was eleven years old, Olson was grown and had moved out of the state looking for work. While it's possible their paths crossed before then, the likelihood of two boys of such different ages being good buddies is slim, although they may have had some contact as adults, either through Olson's work as a prosecutor or through social network ties.

Olson did have friends who were criminals. One of his closest companions, who was at the Mayo Clinic with him when he died and served as a pallbearer at his funeral, was Charlie Ward. Ward had spent time in prison for cocaine possession and was still socially connected to mobsters. However, as far as I am aware, Isadore did not attend Olson's funeral, suggesting the lack of a relationship between them.

Olson had a reputation for being what we would call today "soft on crime" while he was county attorney. He was fundamentally, consistently anti-oppression, which contributed to his refusal to grind defendants into the dust.[80] He served as county attorney from the time of Nash's removal in 1920 through 1930. Olson did abuse his position in some ways, such as by doing favors for friends accused of crimes, but it is doubtful that another man in Olson's situation would have run a cleaner house than he did.[81] The city and county were, at that time, embroiled in an orgy of government and business corruption. Hennepin County Treasurer Henry C. Hanke committed grand larceny. Minneapolis Chief of Police Frank W. Brunskill's involvement with racketeers earned him a grand jury investigation, which was hampered by a witness's refusal to testify. Mayor George E. Leach fired Brunskill—but maybe not because of the grand jury scrutiny. A journalist later said that

Sumner School and the surrounding area, including the North Side neighborhood, 1925. *Courtesy of Hennepin County Library.*

Local corruption: Henry C. Hanke (*far right*), the Hennepin County treasurer, whispering a plea of guilty to grand larceny, 1922. *Courtesy of Hennepin County Library.*

The Foshay Tower nearing completion, 1928. *Courtesy of Hennepin County Library.*

Leach was angry because Brunskill intercepted a bribe intended for the mayor. The Foshay Tower, which dominated the skyline for a long time after its erection in 1928–29, was funded by financial scams.[82] Several years before Olson joined the county attorney's office, the mayor's private secretary was convicted of rape after he paid the parents of a minor to allow him to have sex with her, and the proprietor of a major Minneapolis hotel was caught bribing police officers. The rot ran deep, and Olson, much like Isadore, was a man of his time.

The Rise of the Combination

In 1928 or '29, Isadore and his brothers formed the Minneapolis Combination with Edward "Barney" Berman, who was the same age as Isadore, and Abe Brownstein.[83] Brownstein, a handsome veteran of World War I, was a few years older than Isadore and had served time in Leavenworth for bootlegging whiskey. With his experience, Brownstein was the "brains" of the Combination, and Berman was also highly intelligent.[84] The five men would be close to each other for a long time to come—"like brothers," Barney Berman recalled.[85]

Their main competition came from a man six years Isadore's senior. Thomas Williams "Tommy" Banks, who had moved to Minneapolis in 1920, worked for a short while as head bellboy at the Dyckman Hotel. He provided whiskey to hotel guests and, in this pursuit, earned an absurd daily income of $100 to $200. He used his earnings to fund a bootlegging operation and tapped into Ed Morgan's Irish Syndicate.[86] Banks had a well-established liquor business by then and also had experience in leadership in the army as well as in legitimate, stable salesmanship back in Omaha. A friend of Isadore's told mob historian Paul Maccabee that the Combination and the Syndicate "began clashing head on, hijacking each other's liquor en route from Canada."[87]

The Combination employed a specialist team of hit men, safecrackers, thieves and kidnappers and enjoyed a wide network of freelance suppliers. They held their own, even after Yiddy was charged in 1929 with violating the Prohibition Act and sentenced to the reformatory. He was paroled in September 1930 and allowed to return home.[88]

Perhaps partly because of the bad losses Tommy Banks suffered on the stock market in 1929 (according to a friend of his), he lost interest in fighting

Members of the Elks Club gather to hear the "Great Bambino" Babe Ruth, 1926. Frank W. Brunskill stands second from right; Babe Ruth stands in the middle, next to him. *Courtesy of Hennepin County Library.*

View from the top of the Nicollet Hotel looking toward city hall, 1924. *Courtesy of Hennepin County Library.*

Right: The Hennepin County Grand Jury had its work cut out for it in the 1920s. Here, Hennepin County Deputy Sheriff Johnson guards the grand jury door, 1924. *Courtesy of Hennepin County Library.*

Below: Downtown Minneapolis industrial sprawl, 1925. *Courtesy of Hennepin County Library.*

Above: Donaldson's Glass Block Department Store, 1925. *Courtesy of Hennepin County Library.*

Opposite, top: Downtown street scene, 1928. *Courtesy of Hennepin County Library.*

Opposite, bottom: Construction of the Sears Roebuck Building on Lake Street near Chicago Avenue, 1928. *Courtesy of Hennepin County Library.*

the Combination.[89] Around the time that Yiddy returned to Minneapolis, Banks reached an agreement with Isadore.

Harry Rosenbaum, who was five years younger than Yiddy, recalled the mob he knew as multiethnic, a "combination of the Italians and the Irish and the Jews."[90]

Alvin "Creepy Face" Karpis wrote about the two major bootleggers as if they were partners. He recalled a New Year's Eve 1932 party at the Green Lantern speakeasy in St. Paul where he was "dazzled" by the infamous figures he met there, such as "Tommy Banks and Kid Cann of Minneapolis, who ran alcohol and booze and had the gambling in Excelsior."[91]

Tela Burt, a musician in the 1920s and '30s who would become the first Black real estate agent in the Twin Cities, says that at a club in Excelsior, on Lake Minnetonka, "They had a policeman at the gate, and they had

8320A.

SEARS-ROEBUCK BLDG.
B-W CONSTRUCTION CO.
Minneapolis
12-29-27 No. 37

Above: Looking south on Hennepin Avenue from Sixth Street, 1928. *Courtesy of Hennepin County Library.*

Opposite: Dyckman Hotel, 1922. *Courtesy of Hennepin County Library.*

one when you entered the place. Nobody could get in unless he was a key member." While this was not Isadore's club, it does help us understand how openly such places were allowed to operate, with assistance from the "authorities."

As Burt explained, key clubs were "nothin' but millionaire clubs where guys brought their secretaries…and those guys had all the liquor you could think of. They even played roulette out there, had gambling and everything." Burt would "play all night on Saturday nights [at the Excelsior club on Lake Minnetonka]. I'd come back with thirty or forty dollars in my pocket Sunday morning. And they had a whole gang of them places. They had one down there in South St. Paul. They had another one about twenty miles south of St. Paul."

On the North Side of Minneapolis, Isadore owned at least three clubs. "We just called it 'Sixth and Lyndale North,' that's all," said Burt. "Downstairs

they had a luncheon, and upstairs they had the dance hall. Cann used to come and sit right in front of the orchestra. He used to give us tips. He had a lot of money."[92]

There was serious cash in bootlegging, and once the network was established, it was so simple that even a child could do it. Rosenbaum was only fourteen when he got started.

Three men inspecting liquor bottles for the case to revoke the licenses of North Minneapolis's Stables Nightclub, 1928. *Courtesy of Hennepin County Library.*

One of my buddies had an older brother that was working for the Combination. He said, "How would you like to make some extra money? I said, "Sure"—not "What?" but "Sure." He said, "When you're out delivering, deliver some packages for me." I said, "Great." He said, "Two bits apiece...right in the neighborhood." I did that for maybe three months or so. And [then] *I said, "You know what? I've got some buddies, some friends, that would like some of this, too. I want a cut for it." So he said, "Sure, for you, it's a different price. You get the wholesale price." I did that for about six months.*

Then we went over to Wisconsin once, and we were able to buy some stuff called Ever-Kleer, which is 200-proof alcohol. We cut that so there was about 20 percent. Now, 200 proof is pure.... [Scotch] *will usually be 80 proof. So this is two and a half times as strong. So we cut it so that it was milder, and we found out that the young guys, my guy's buddies, didn't like it real strong. So we cut it down a little bit more. The more we cut it, the better it was. We used Glenwood Inglewood water.*

> *There was a guy named Moshe that I had been buying booze from before. He was making it, but he would sell it to me to use, like a half a pint or a pint at a time. He told me how to make the caramel color by burning sugar. I could buy the scotch and bourbon flavors from him. He charged me a fortune, but it was worth it.*[93]

Abe Brownstein would later tell FBI agents that he, Isadore and Barney Berman "were considered by the Federal government as the biggest alcohol peddlers in the country as they used to deal in alcohol by the carload."[94] Figures of folklore can participate in their own mythmaking.

Dr. Albert Fried, history professor at the State University of New York, wrote of Isadore, Harry, Yiddy "and their confederates" in almost mystical terms. Prohibition, he said, was like a deus ex machina. Isadore and company, who had been

> *tempered by constant struggle, for their neighborhood was enclosed by a particularly vicious anti-Semitism…rose aggressively to the challenge of Prohibition, as though the deus ex machina had addressed them specifically.…Kid Cann was a power to reckon with throughout the upper Mississippi region and beyond.*[95]

Chapter 3

ISADORE ON THE ROAD

Risky Business

Sleepy farming communities faced major social upheaval from the forces of Prohibition. Families who had been brewing or distilling alcoholic beverages for their own consumption since before they came over from the Old Country suddenly found that this traditional practice could generate an income. They sure needed it. Farmers in much of Minnesota were struggling in the 1920s. During World War I, the federal government encouraged farmers to grow more produce, so they borrowed money to cover the costs of land and equipment. Then the war ended, and the European countries that, before, had imported produce could no longer afford to do so, mired in their own debts. U.S. farmers, in turn, could not pay their debts.[96] When gangsters came knocking, many farm families jumped at the bait. There was a lot of bait.

Bootleggers came from all over the Midwest to Stearns County, Minnesota, to buy Minnesota 13, which was said to be comparable to Canadian Club whiskey. They came from Chicago. They came from Kansas City. And of course, they came from Minneapolis and St. Paul. Isadore and his brothers were frequent visitors and were said to own land in the area, but when a vicious, downright sadistic Prohibition enforcement operation broke the network behind Minnesota 13, Isadore was nowhere in sight.[97]

The farmland itself was valuable, even if the farmers themselves were not involved with moonshining.

Theodore Kinkor, a Wright County farmer, was approached by Billy Schmalek, who introduced him to a man who called himself John Hanson.

Hanson was an agent for Isadore. They wanted to buy some farmland from Kinkor, and in the spring of 1929, Kinkor sold his farm to Hanson. Hanson agreed to pay Kinkor $6,000: $1,000 right away and $5,000 more later. That's approximately $18,000 that Kinkor got up front, in today's dollars, with about $93,000 on the horizon. Isadore hired a cooker, Frank "Finney" Phillips, to operate a distillery that was put up in a brick house on the farm. Phillips, Hanson and another man ran it. In the basement, they stuck five-hundred-gallon vats for mash, a mix of older batch with new batch to stimulate fermentation. They kept the still in the kitchen. Kinkor didn't live there anymore. He was staying at his mother's home on an adjoining farm, but he did visit, and he sampled the liquor and saw the setup.

One day in June that year, Edward Quast was working in his cornfield in Arlington Township, Sibley County, when two men drove up to his property. One of them, a swarthy young man, got out of the car, while the other man stayed inside. The young man walked over to Quast. He introduced himself as Jerry Meyers and expressed an interest in renting a log barn on Quast's property. They reached an agreement: Meyers would pay $150 (about $2,800 today) per month to use the barn to house a distillery. Meyers paid the first month's rent around the time that they moved in. Meyers and the other man visited multiple times and, on top of the rent for the barn, paid Quast for room and board for their cookers in the distillery. The cookers lived in the family home, and Mrs. Quast and her twelve-year-old daughter served them at mealtimes.

John D. Hunt drove a tank wagon for the Arlington Oil Company, owned by his father and brother. Isadore, who was in fact the man who called himself Meyers, arranged for Hunt to supply gasoline for the distillery and brought empty gasoline drums as well. Isadore, who was usually accompanied by that other man (whom law enforcement came to believe was Abe Brownstein) paid Hunt in cash for deliveries.

On January 26, 1931, Hunt was questioned by the Prohibition administrator in St. Paul, M.L. Harney. Asked to identify photographs of other suspected violators in his network, Hunt pointed to a picture of Isadore and said, "This here one looks like him." He also picked out another man, Abe Brownstein, although he was less sure of the second identification.

An indictment was returned on March 2 against Isadore and Brownstein and a few more men for conspiracy to transport "railroad carload shipments of alcohol from Trenton, New Jersey, or North Philadelphia, Pennsylvania, during the latter part of 1929, to Arlington, Minnesota."[98] By the time of the indictment, the alcohol was long gone.

Hank Larson was a night guard at the Gateway Garage in Minneapolis. He observed that a white truck was frequently brought to the garage. A few days before Easter Sunday, April 5, 1931, a man named Ray Miller came to the garage and drove off with an International truck. He came back towing the white truck, which had broken down. Sitting in the white truck were Abe Brownstein and two other men. A whole bunch of other guys drove up in cars. They parked outside and stood around. Brownstein had a revolver. The men all left, but the truck stayed. On Easter morning, Larson realized that the truck was loaded with alcohol (more than 1,050 gallons, as it turned out), and he reported it to the authorities.[99]

Learning about the operation at the Kinkor farm, Prohibition agents went there on June 23. They found no distillery, but there was evidence that one had been there. Kinkor and one of the cookers explained the operation to the agents.

Isadore and Brownstein would have gone to trial in June 1931 if the prosecution in the Quast farm case had been ready for the general term of court in Mankato. But both men were in New Orleans at the time. Isadore came up with bail for appearance at the next term of court. In September, indictments were returned against Brownstein, Larson and all the other men who could be linked to the white truck incident at the Gateway Garage. Witnesses in the Kinkor farm case had to testify before a grand jury in November. The jurors refused to indict anyone except for Isadore, against whom they returned an indictment for possession of a distillery, and Isadore had to put up more money as bond in his absence.

The grand jury in Mankato subpoenaed Edward Quast. He was granted immunity. At that time, he was "quite positive" about his version of events, but "he became weaker as time went on." Investigators heard a rumor that the conspirators or their associates had visited Mr. and Mrs. Quast and their daughter and threatened them "so that they would have lapses of memory if the case was ever brought on for trial."

Prohibition agents got word that some of the "racketeers" were on their way to the Quast farm again and drove out to stop them, but they were too late. There were multiple visits, the authorities never caught them in the act and "the Quasts became more fearful."[100]

In the spring of 1932, the case against Kinkor was presented again to the grand jury. This time, it returned an indictment. Kinkor had never met Isadore. He had never seen Isadore. The government hoped to get Phillips to cooperate. He had a history of snitching. Ernest J. Meili, Minneapolis probation officer, said he had been told that Isadore, Brownstein and associates were planning to kill Phillips. He let Phillips leave town but told him that he had to stay in touch. "This was done so as to avert any catastrophe with regard to Finney Phillips."[101] Phillips did not stay in touch and was unavailable to testify against Isadore.

In October, the charges against Isadore in the Kinkor farm case were nolled in Hennepin County, where his case had been transferred. A few days later, he was found guilty in a St. Paul federal court of conspiracy to violate the National Prohibition Act in regard to the railroad shipments of alcohol and fined $1,500. That was barely anything to him.

Referring to all these investigations at the Kinkor farm, the Quast farm and the Gateway Garage, U.S. Attorney Lewis L. Drill wrote,

> *The cases against Isadore Blumenfeld, who was the leader of this racketeering crowd, were, of course, the weakest as heretofore referred to. In the Quast farm matter the Quasts would have been very hesitant and doubtless when pressed would not have been sure of their identification of Blumenfeld. In the Kinkor farm case we had no witness to identify Blumenfeld. In the conspiracy case* [regarding transportation of liquor to Arlington] *there was no evidence in the way of liquor seized and the Government would have been hard pressed to go to trial and to prove that charge against the defendant Blumenfeld. These cases had been pending for a considerable length of time. The evidence was cold, through no fault of the Prohibition* [agents] *as they had put forth great effort to run Isadore Blumenfeld alias Kid Cann to earth. As in all such cases, however, he working through many intermediaries, the farmers who did have some knowledge being afraid and hesitant, and the information coming to* [investigators] *so long after the violations occurred, it would have been difficult to obtain a conviction against Isadore Blumenfeld. His henchmen, of course, would never give any information against him.*[102]

The crux of the Combination's business was a legitimate-sounding company, La Pompadour, a perfume manufacturer. This was a front for the legal importation from Canada of industrial-grade alcohol. Some of it was used for its ostensible purpose as "barbershop supply" materials, but nearly all the alcohol was for eventual drinking. The liquor produced by the Combination was sold in Minnesota and to Al Capone's Outfit in Chicago, although it had buyers in other states as well.[103]

The full extent of Isadore's sales network will never be known, but Prohibition agents found evidence of the Combination making liquor business deals with persons located in Norwood, in Carver County; Mankato; Moorhead; Fargo, North Dakota; Grand Forks, North Dakota; East Grand Forks in Polk County, Minnesota; Cleveland, in Sueur County, Minnesota; and Dundas, in Rice County.[104]

Stories from family lore give us some sense of Isadore's presence. *Volsteadland* podcast host Amy Lotsberg heard from one of her listeners in 2021, "My grandfather worked for Kid Cann running moonshine and making it.…He was told by Cann that he had to [take the fall] or something would happen to his family when the Feds raided my grandfather's house." The family kept chickens, so "my grandfather poured the mash from making the booze [where the chickens could get it], and the chickens ate the mash, and they got drunken chickens walking around. The Feds destroyed the still, and [my grandfather] went to jail." Lotsberg recalled that she asked if "Kid Cann ever repaid her grandfather for taking the fall for him and she said nope."[105]

There was the obvious risk of running afoul of the authorities, as well as the risk of running afoul of gangsters, but brushing up against the underworld in this way brought its own reward in the form of excitement. In her family history, *The Hammonds of Lilydale: Life of Edward Delos Hammond and His Children*, Deanna Marie Huston shares tales about "Uncle George," who homesteaded in Wisconsin in the 1920s. He would travel to Lilydale in Dakota County, Minnesota, to visit family and to traffic the moonshine he produced on his farm, which he sold to the Combination. "One of Uncle George's thank you[s] from 'Mr. Kid Cann' himself was to play poker with him and Uncle George's nephew…at the Mystic Night Club that was in the mushroom caves in Lilydale."[106]

I have heard accounts of Isadore operating in nearly every region of Minnesota, which reflects if not the true extent of his empire at least that of his reputation. Family legend is a mixed bag from a historian's perspective. While I was researching this book, people generously shared with me bootlegging stories from their parents and grandparents that are verifiably untrue. They are not without value, as they tell us how Isadore was viewed and how he is remembered.

Some families are faced with the opposite problem: physical evidence without the context of a story. Mrs. Abe Brownstein's cabin in Detroit Lakes, Becker County, was found, after her death, to contain evidence of bootlegging operations. However, says her granddaughter, Sandra Brownstein, "everything was kind of a big secret." Her grandparents had told her nothing of their family's criminal history during Prohibition.[107]

Isadore in the Big Easy

At 9:10 one night in late March 1931, Isadore placed a call from his temporary home in apartment 1-A, Jackson Apartments, New Orleans to Austin F. McFee, with whom he'd been doing business. Even among people known to him, he had been using his brother Harry's name.

McFee: Hello.
Isadore: Mac?
McFee: Yeah. Harry?
Isadore: Say, Mac, I wouldn't go up there in the country if I were you. You know what I mean.
McFee: I'm not going up there.
Isadore: I thought I would tell you, as there is going to be five of those eggs up there for a couple of days.
McFee: I'm going to work a little tonight.
Isadore: Well, that's alright, just so you don't go up there. I'll see you tomorrow and have a talk with you.
McFee: Alright, Harry. Thanks.[108]

They were obviously speaking in code, on the off chance that Bureau of Prohibition investigators were listening in on their calls. This type of caution was a feature of the gangster life.[109] This conversation was but one of many that Prohibition agents overheard, some of them vaguely ominous, such as an exchange they listened to between Isadore and an accomplice, Albert M. Morrison, who called to reach someone else but talked to Isadore instead:

Morrison: Joe?
Isadore: Joe is not in. This is Harry.
Morrison: Bert speaking. I'm going out for a while. Did the boys get back?
Isadore: Didn't make it 100%, but almost.
Morrison: That's good.[110]

There could be a fine line between "code" and "a waste of investigators' time." On March 20, 1931, McFee called Morry Roisner, a Minnesota confederate of Isadore's:

Roisner: Hello.
McFee: Say, Morry, I sold Harry 400 oysters yesterday. Is that alright?

> *Roisner: Sure.*
> *McFee: I don't know what to do about packing that stuff.*
> *Roisner: Better see "you know." He can tell you about it. I think you can go ahead. I'll guarantee the account.*
> *McFee: I just wanted you to call him and tell him the sale is alright.*
> *Roisner: Alright, Mac.*[111]

That's a helluva lot of oysters, assuming that they really were oysters.

On October 27, 1931, Special Agent R.E. Herrick wrote a letter to the director of the Bureau of Prohibition in New Orleans, enclosing his report on Case 236-S. He described therein extensive investigative efforts involving Prohibition agents from New Orleans, Detroit, San Francisco, Florida and New York, as well as a customs inspector and customs agents in Louisiana, Mississippi, Minneapolis, St. Paul, San Francisco, Belize, British Honduras, Vancouver, Victoria, Detroit, New York City, Cleveland and two towns in Connecticut.

There were twenty-two suspects in the case, an alleged conspiracy to violate the National Prohibition Act. Herrick explained,

> *The investigation of this case disclosed that rum smuggling into the United States in the Gulf area during the period from May, 1930, to April 11, 1931, was, for the most part, controlled by the Consolidated Exporters Corporation, Limited, and its subsidiary companies and affiliations of Vancouver, British Columbia, through its branch at Belize, British Honduras, its branch at Montreal, Quebec, and their local representative at New Orleans, Louisiana, with the various bootleg liquor syndicates and racketeering organizations consisting of known Chicago liquor violators, known New York City liquor violators, who operated in connection with known New Orleans liquor violators.*

Investigators seized a metric ton of documentary evidence.

> *A recapitulation of the accounts found in the possession of A*[lbert] *M. Morrison disclosed that during the period from May 10, 1930, to March 25, 1931, the Consolidated Exporters Corporation, Limited, through its branch at Belize, British Honduras, shipped 56,745 cases of assorted liquors on various boats operating under their control or under charter by* [the defendants]….*The records disclosed that forty such boat trips were made during this period; that the in-voices covering the sale of the*

> *56,745 cases showed a total of sales in the amount of $961,703.17, which is an average of $16.94 per case, representing the wholesale cost price per case delivered f.o.b.* [fresh off the boat], *in the vicinity of the twelve mile territorial limits of the United States in the Gulf area. The records further disclosed that the said liquor was re-sold by the defendants at an average sale price of $40.00 per case, or a total of $2,269,720.00* [approximately $46 million today].

Austin F. McFee had made the sales between May 20, 1930, and September 30, 1930; A.M. Morrison, from whom the records were confiscated, had taken over McFee's role.

The Consolidated Exporters Corporation (CEC) was not a shell company or a crime syndicate. As of 1932, it had 1.2 million authorized shares of stock, of which 1,030,007 had been issued in cash at a dollar a share. The CEC had legitimate business in the Gulf, where it shipped liquor from Scotland; Halifax, Nova Scotia; St. Pierre and Miquelon; and Vancouver, British Columbia, to a CEC branch in Belize, "where it was placed in their storage warehouses and subsequently re-shipped via rum boats to various positions in the Gulf of Mexico in close proximity of the twelve mile territorial limit." There, smaller boats would meet the ship, load the rum and then follow a course up the rivers and bayous. After that, the rum was transferred to cars, trucks or freight cars and sent to Chicago, Cleveland and other north central locations.

> *Other foreign liquor companies such as Hiram Walker's Distillery, Pioneer Distillers and United Traders, kept a supply of their brands at Belize… in the custody of the Melhado brothers, who acted as agents for most foreign liquor companies, with the exception of the Consolidated Exporters Corporation, Limited, and purchases made by the various bootleg interests in the United States containing brands other than those of the Consolidated Exporters, would be supplied by the Melhado brothers and delivered to the Consolidated Exporters' branch at Belize to be included in shipments going forth from the Consolidated Exporters' branch.*

The bootlegging proceeded much like legitimate sales would.

> *The method of operation of the Consolidated Exporters in the delivery of their merchandise, after Morrison received the orders for same, would be for him to notify the Belize branch and the main office of the Consolidated*

Exporters Corporation, Limited, at Vancouver, B.C., the orders being verified by the Vancouver office to the Belize office by either radiograms, cablegrams or telegrams.

Behind it all, "The movements of the various rum ships operating out of Belize, B.H., in the interests of the Consolidated Exporters Corporation, Limited, were controlled and directed by A.M. Morrison." He mostly used "a radio communicating system through a station located at New Orleans, Louisiana, and one located at Belize."

Herrick and his team had plenty of evidence, as they had made "large seizures of smuggled liquors…at various times…said seizures consisting of contact boats, luggers, speedboats and freight car shipments," and had managed to trace "the ownership of all of the seized liquors" to the defendants.[112]

Isadore ("alias Harry Bloom, Joe Miller, the Kid, Kid Kahn, J.B. Moore, J.B. Miller, M. Miller") was arrested on April 11, 1931, in New Orleans. He was released on a $10,000 bond while he awaited the grand jury.[113]

Herrick described the thirty-year-old bootlegger as "a known liquor violator…implicated in the purchase of several automobiles and trucks which were used in transporting liquor."[114] In his apartment, investigators found documentation directly linking him to the sales, as well as some "intoxicating liquor." In addition, a bookkeeper working for the operation had agreed to give testimony implicating Isadore. All the same, Isadore tried to bluff. "This defendant," wrote Herrick, "at the time of his arrest, was shown all of the evidence taken from [his apartment], and asked if any of [it] belonged to him, to which he replied that he knew nothing about it and that none of it belonged to him."[115]

As it turned out, that was a smart move. On June 11, 1932, an order issued by the U.S. District Court, Eastern District of Louisiana, New Orleans Division granted a motion filed on behalf of Isadore and his roommate "to quash the search warrant issued herein and to suppress the evidence and return to defendants the property seized under said warrant." Albert M. Morrison was similarly fortunate.

It's not as if Isadore was there to celebrate: he had skipped town months earlier, failing to appear at trial on charges of conspiring to violate the National Prohibition Act, the Radio Act and the Tariff Act. He faced no consequences for that at the time, nor would he ever. He did not return to Louisiana.

In a move that must have enraged some of the investigators, A.W.W. Woodcock, special assistant to the attorney general of the United States, recommended to Assistant Attorney General Keenan on June 13, 1934, that "each of these indictments [regarding the New Orleans bootlegging case] be nol prossed. The events happened in the Spring of 1931. There had been one trial. The Eighteenth Amendment has been repealed." The jurors in that trial had not had their hearts in it, as they demonstrated by drinking two bottles of evidence. "I doubt if it is even remotely possible now to secure a conviction," wrote Woodcock.[116] Keenan concurred.

Squared

In August 1932, Austin Cravath, a filling station manager, and Conrad "Con" Althen, a former golf course manager, set up a moonshining operation. On April Fool's Day the following year, Althen told Cravath that he had made "arrangements for them, with others whom he did not name." These "others" provided Cravath and Althen with plants that could rectify more than six hundred gallons of alcohol in a single day and sent trucks to "haul alcohol to the plants and to haul rectified spirits away from the plants." Austin's son Calvert was a teenager then, and when he was an old man, he recalled making moonshine with his dad on the Dexheimer farm near Mendota. "You wore shorts and tennis shoes, with sweat rolling off you." To prevent hijacking, men with submachine guns guarded the farm, and they sometimes hijacked liquor from other operations. "We were so big, that [once] one of our semi trucks left, the call [alarm signal] went off, and our hijackers hijacked our own stuff!" They made protection payments at Fort Snelling and bribed local law enforcement officials with whiskey. This allowed Austin Cravath to get tipped off about police raids. Stills in active use would be hidden with blankets; a couple of others would be destroyed by policemen with axes as reporters watched. Once the newsmen had gone, the broken stills would be replaced with two new ones from a Minneapolis warehouse.[117]

Althen was now bookkeeping for the Combination, those mysterious "others." He used a black loose-leaf ledger, about three by six inches in size. Austin Cravath would tell Althen how many drums of specially denatured alcohol had been brought to him and how many gallons of finished alcohol were taken away by truck. Althen would take notes on slips of paper that he stuck into the ledger. Two weeks after he started, Althen had a new book, much larger, about ten by twelve inches, bound in leather. "Business has increased so rapidly that I had to get another book," he told Cravath.

Fort Snelling, 1924. *Courtesy of Hennepin County Library.*

In June, Austin Cravath told Alfred Dexheimer to rent the Wilson brothers' farm on Normandale Avenue in Edina Township. Dexheimer paid the rent for one month, with money that Cravath gave him. They were moving the still on Dexheimer's home farm to the Wilson farm. Dexheimer and Cravath unloaded twenty-one drums of alcohol from a truck. Dexheimer was starting to set up stoves and make various other preparations for the distillery when an Edina constable arrested him. He was brought to the Hennepin County Jail in Minneapolis, where he stayed for several days. Attorney Archie Cary showed up and "told him everything was all right."[118] Dexheimer appeared before a judge the next day, pleaded guilty to a nuisance charge and was fined one hundred dollars. Cary paid it for him.

Bootlegging was in its final hour. On February 20, Congress had proposed an amendment to repeal Prohibition. It was sent out for ratification to state conventions. The writing was on the wall. Gangsters would have to start looking for other ways to make money. Kidnapping wealthy people for ransom fit the bill—wealthy people like oilman Charles Urschel.

On July 22, 1933, Urschel was at home in Oklahoma City, playing bridge on the screened-in porch with his friend Walter Jarrett and their wives, when they were interrupted by George "Machine Gun" Kelly Barnes and his partner, Albert L. Bates. In front of the frightened women, Barnes and Bates kidnapped the men at gunpoint. Urschel was their target. Urschel, once widowed, had married a wealthy woman. He was already rich in his own right, and the two of them together were "one of the wealthiest couples in Oklahoma City."[119]

Barnes and his confederates allowed Mr. Jarrett to go, and then they brought Urschel to a farmhouse. He was blindfolded but observed his surroundings as best he could, noting, for example, the timing of airplane flights overhead. J. Edgar Hoover interested himself in the case. Urschel was released after the receipt of the $200,000 ransom, and Hoover's agents

were able to use Urschel's descriptions of the setting to locate the house in Paradise, Texas, where he had been held.

Investigators searched the belongings of Kathryn, Kelly's wife, and found the phone number of one of Isadore's associates, Jack Peifer (also Pfeifer or Pfeiffer), who managed the Hollyhocks casino at 1590 South Mississippi River Boulevard in St. Paul.

In August, some of the ransom money appeared at the Hennepin Avenue Branch of the First National Bank, from people with some connection to the members of the Combination. They said they got the cash from Barney Berman. Another man involved with the Combination also took some of the ransom money to the First National Bank. When he was caught, he told investigators that he got it from yet another guy, and that guy said he got it from Barney Berman.

Around the time that Althen started keeping their books, the Combination moved into headquarters at the West Hotel, where Mark Twain and Winston Churchill stayed when they visited Minneapolis in time gone by. Isadore, Barney Berman, Brownstein, Tommy Banks and a few of their associates occupied rooms 728 and 730. Their typical room service order was ginger ale or mineral water.

On August 3, a man "from the south" appeared at the West Hotel. He spoke to Barney Berman about his desire to buy liquor. Berman "turned this man over to…Blumenfeld, because he had southern connections."[120] Their associate Clifford Skelly was there as well. The man gave Isadore $5,500 in $20 bills.[121] That was the story Isadore and company would give to investigators to explain how they got that cash.

The FBI would later write,

> *It is common knowledge in Minneapolis that* [prior to] *August 8, 1933…a substantial amount of the URSCHEL kidnapping money was at Hub Schueller's Saloon in Golden Valley, a suburb of Minneapolis, in*

> *the possession of the following individuals, who were planning to dispose of it in Minneapolis:*
>
> *ISADORE BLUMENFIELD, wa. Kid Cann*
> *EDWARD BERMAN, wa. Barney Berman*
> *CLIFFORD SKELLY*
> *ISADORE WOLK*
> *ARCHIE CAREY (Minneapolis criminal attorney)*
> *JOSEPH LEHMEYER*[122]

On August 8, Special Agent R.C. Coulter of the Division of Investigation, U.S. Department of Justice, went to the West Hotel, but Isadore and his partners weren't there. The newspapers broke the story that evening that investigators had information about the ransom money, including that it was paid in twenty-dollar bills.[123]

Seventeen days later, Isadore was indicted along with Barney Berman, Clifford Skelly and three other men for "conspiracy in connection with the kidnapping of Charles F. Urschel."[124] In the language of the indictment, they "did knowingly, wilfully and unlawfully possess, conceal and exchange approximately Five Thousand Five Hundred Dollars ($5,500.00) of the original ransom money paid to the…conspirators for the release of… Chas. F. Urschel."[125]

The Division of Investigation in St. Paul arrested Isadore, Berman, Skelly and codefendants. Werner Hanni, the head of the division, contacted another field office to ask them to forward the paperwork for holding the arrestees. The paperwork arrived, but it was "found defective," and Hanni was told that the men could not be held. They were released but rearrested. Several of them said, "I thought this case had been squared."[126]

Joseph Lehmeyer, Minneapolis chief of police, said later that the defendants had surrendered themselves to him and then were brought to St. Paul. But on the way, some of the arrestees showed the assembled newsmen that they had not surrendered in spirit. Barney Berman tried to "sprint out of the focus of the camera." Most defiant of all was Isadore, who "wav[ed] a newspaper as he attempted to swat a newspaper photographer."[127]

Agent Coulter interviewed the defendants once they were in custody. He asked Isadore where he was on August 8 when Coulter went to the West Hotel and found him absent. Isadore replied that in the morning, he was at a golf course, and in the afternoon, he was in Medicine Lake, meeting with his lawyers. He said the reason he went to Medicine Lake was that "he knew he would be picked up if he stayed in Minneapolis," Coulter

J. Edgar Hoover, 1924. *Library of Congress Prints and Photographs Division.*

testified at the kidnapping trial. "He told me that he knew we were looking for him, and he wanted to talk to his attorneys."[128] Isadore, Skelly, Berman and Tommy Banks, so they said, all went golfing together and then went to talk to their lawyers at Medicine Lake. Coulter could not find Banks to ask him about this.

On September 13, Calvert Cravath's brother Morton drove with their father to the Nelson farm. Austin drove to Minneapolis in the afternoon, but Morton stayed on the farm. When his father did not come back that evening, Morton went to sleep on a cot on the back porch of the Nelsons' house.

After midnight, Morton was woken up by men walking around the farm—about a dozen of them, including Conrad Althen. There was a truck by the cement garage that held the distillery. Some of the men were loading fifty-five-gallon drums of alcohol onto the truck; others stood around watching. Althen told Morton that "his father…had been picked up and that they were going to move the stuff out." Mr. Nelson "seemed rather excited, and kept running about the premises."[129]

The men loaded about twenty-five drums and then drove over to the granary, where they loaded two thousand gallons of alcohol in one-gallon tins onto the truck. They drove off toward the road. The truck was so heavily loaded that as it went up the grade, the front wheels lifted off the ground a few times.

Althen left and came back with another truck, and they loaded what remained: seven hundred gallons in one-gallon tins. They disconnected the stills, and then all the men drove off into the night.

Five days after that, the Urschel kidnapping trial opened in Oklahoma City. For Isadore, one of the worst moments of the trial may have been when a witness who was asked to point to George Bates, the kidnapper, mistakenly identified "defendant Blumenfeld."[130] But his defense team launched a thorough offensive. Among the witnesses they subpoenaed was Chief Joseph Lehmeyer himself. At the time of the indictment, Lehmeyer had been chief of police for only a month and a half, although he was a career cop before that. He would be demoted to captain in the wake of the trial, but it wasn't as if he revealed anything damaging to himself or the department. One element of the Kid Cann myth is that he was so powerful that the chief of police rushed out to Oklahoma to testify on his behalf, as if he were doing a favor for a pal. The biggest issue is probably how close Lehmeyer's collusion with the underworld came to the surface prior to the trial. The worst that came out in Lehmeyer's cross-examination was his admittance that he had known Berman and Isadore for "about six or seven years" and that he had known Clifford Skelly for longer.[131]

Isadore, unlike most of his co-conspirators, was acquitted of all charges. Lehmeyer, it goes without saying, faced no legal consequences at all.

IN NOVEMBER THAT YEAR, investigators seized a freight car full of alcohol. Not long after that, federal agents stopped Isadore on the highway near Minneapolis. One of them said to him, "That was some hard luck, losing that carload of alcohol."

Isadore replied, "What are you talking about?"

"Didn't that carload of alcohol belong to you?"

"You know better than to ask me questions like that and expect me to say anything." Isadore added, "You can have the racket. For the last two months it has been terrible." This was a lie. The two months after the Urschel trial had been very lucrative for the Combination, and Isadore had a lot to lose.[132]

Chapter 4

GETTING AWAY WITH MURDER?

Unhappy Mischance

M.L. Harney wrote in 1956 to George E. MacKinnon, U.S. attorney for the District of Minnesota,

> *Investigator Cleo Hitsman, a Deputy Marshal and I went to Althen's house early one morning to arrest him on a warrant. When the Deputy Marshal didn't think force was appropriate we posted him at the rear while we proceeded to break in the front. Althen, a good athlete, dove out the back window over the fat marshal's head—by unhappy mischance, for him and us—he managed to flag a passing motorist and disappeared. Search of the premises disclosed some fragmentary accounting records indicating that he was a bookkeeper for the Combination, a fact of which we had some prior knowledge....*
>
> *Shortly afterwards* [on the night of December 18, 1933] *Althen's body was found in Dakota County....The "street" gossip as it subsequently came to me and which I believe to be correct is that Althen went to see some of his principals, discussed the fact that we were after him, and suggested that he be given expenses to get out of town, specifically to go to Florida. As the story goes, this was entirely agreeable to the principals. However, when* [Althen] *indicated a figure for his expenses which the boys thought was entirely out of line the mob was greatly displeased at what might have been construed as blackmail. So when the unsuspecting Althen showed up for the pay-off it was with bullets....*

> *Con had made no offer to us to be a government witness, but I am convinced that the fear that he would become one or the threat that he would become one was the reason for his murder.*[133]

On December 5, 1933, the day the Eighteenth Amendment was repealed and Prohibition ended, a federal grand jury in St. Paul indicted Isadore, Barney Berman and Abe Brownstein on charges of a liquor conspiracy. All three men, said the *St. Paul Dispatch*, were "described by the government as 'big shots.'" A little over two weeks later, on December 21, they surrendered themselves at the St. Paul federal district court. Isadore and friends seemed to take it in stride and "appeared much at their ease. They good naturedly parried questions from newspaper men and referred them to A.M. Cary, Minneapolis attorney, for answer." The *Dispatch* noted, "All three were attired nattily in dark suits and did not shy away from photographers as [Isadore and Berman] did when they were arrested in the Urschel case." Cary told the press that his clients "have a conscience free from any connection with [the Althen] killing." Tommy Banks, he said, would soon turn himself in as well.

While Isadore waited for the posting of his $5,000 bond, he told reporters that he "certainly didn't know anything" about Althen's murder. Cary belittled the charge against the men, which concerned the operation of the still that Cravath had managed: "This is the 'big combine' and the 'huge alcohol ring' you have been hearing about." Isadore interjected, "We have lived in Minneapolis all our lives and have families here." He challenged his listeners, "Do you think we would go in for such a thing as [the murder of Con Althen]? Don't be silly. That isn't our line."[134]

Three days later, on Christmas Eve, agents from the Department of Justice raided a Minneapolis apartment that they had learned was "recently occupied by Althen as a headquarters and business office for the 'combination.'" They found key documentary evidence: "a complete index to the books of the ring, some of the ledgers and account books, correspondence, freight and truck waybills, and various other records."[135]

Considering the breadth of Isadore and his codefendants' operations, the charges against them were minimal. The indictment put forth that Althen, along with Austin Cravath, "rented a Mendota farmhouse basement for a still" and that stills were set up on three other farms, in Edina, Crystal and Plymouth. The defendants were charged with "conspiracy to refine denatured alcohol without paying a rectifier's tax, handling liquor shipped from eastern points in large quantities by freight and truck, and removing

4,400 gallons of distilled spirits from a freight car in the Minneapolis, Northfield and Southern railway yards, April 27, 1933."[136] The state had sixty-one witnesses lined up.

It should have been a slam-dunk case, but the prosecuting attorney explained to the court on March 13, 1934, that the government's case had "crumbled." No one was eager to testify anymore. Not after what happened to Althen.

Judge Nordbye nolled cases against the bit players. Seven main characters, including Tommy Banks, Isadore, Brownstein and Barney Berman, pleaded guilty. Banks was fined. Brownstein was fined. Berman was sentenced to a year and a day in Leavenworth. Isadore was sentenced to one year in the Minneapolis workhouse. Attorney Cary, "taking a huge roll of bills from his pocket," paid everyone's fines.[137]

On April 14, 1934, Isadore was incarcerated.[138]

Con Althen's murder remains unsolved.

The First Journalist

Three journalists would meet violent fates in gang-riddled Minneapolis. Isadore was convicted of none of their murders, and he was arrested and tried for only one. However, in the modern-day popular imagination, Isadore became the murderer of all three.[139]

In late summer 1934, Howard Guilford "announced a series of radio talks to 'tell the truth about Governor Floyd Olson's connection with the underworld.'"[140] Shortly after that announcement, on September 6, 1934, Guilford was shot to death during his morning commute. Lehmeyer "investigated," along with another corrupt cop. They, unsurprisingly, did not solve the murder. Isadore was not the gunman. He had an alibi—he was still in the workhouse. While he was capable of arranging a hit, there is nothing to suggest that Guilford was on his radar. Any connection between Isadore and this particular death is purely mythological.

The Alibi Barber

Governor Olson understood the power of the press to shape public opinion. He had a coterie of media-savvy friends. At the Minneapolis Athletic Club, he was introduced to Walter Liggett, a Minnesota-born newsman who had involved himself in progressive causes in different parts of the country for years but had returned from out of state with his family. His two children, Wallace and Marda, were in elementary school, and his wife, Edith, had worked as a reporter for a socialist newspaper. Olson and Liggett came up with a plan for Liggett to run a Farmer-Labor paper in Rochester, and Olson quickly fronted the cash to purchase a decrepit provincial plant and press.

The *Mid-West American*, as the Liggetts dubbed their new publication, was a weekly paper that covered feminist causes, conservation, slum conditions in the cities and workers' welfare. The family moved to Rochester, where they lived happily for a while. The *Mid-West American* was a pro-Olson paper, as was the *Austin American*, a second paper that the Liggetts published under the same agreement. Yet Walter had vigorous disputes with Olson, as he did with many people. Walter debated with his allies and friends vigorously, even obnoxiously; that was the way he was. The clouds had not gathered enough to cover the sun. That was about to change.

The Minneapolis Teamster strike that came in May 1934 took a lot out of Olson. His health had been bad for as long as he had been in state office, both worsened by and worsening his job stress. Minnesota had been in terrible shape not only during the Depression but also before it. Because the economy of the state was so bound up in agriculture, the post–World War I agricultural depression affected the cities, too. Through the 1920s, "anyone who took the time to look closely at what was happening beneath the surface of urban life...could tell that all was not right in Minneapolis and St. Paul"—and throughout the state, really.[141] Flour production in the Mill City declined by 44 percent between 1916 and 1930. Unemployment was a chronic problem, and "in 1926 alone, the Union City Mission in Minneapolis provided lodging to more than fifty-two thousand men."[142]

Minneapolis had never bothered to make it a priority to ameliorate the poverty already in its midst. A local welfare officer remarked, "It has been said that one half of the world doesn't know how the other half lives.... The...half is now learning about the other half through the bitter cup of experience."[143]

The Minneapolis and St. Paul municipal governments spent so much money to provide food and shelter for their residents that there was talk of bankruptcy. Governor Olson fought tooth and nail against an obstructionist state legislature to get authorization for President Roosevelt's New Deal

Minneapolis Athletic Club, 1915. *Courtesy of Hennepin County Library.*

public works projects in Minnesota. His political enemies would accuse him of using construction projects to give jobs to Farmer-Labor Party members, but the evidence indicates that Olson resisted the efforts of party bosses to replace qualified employees appointed under the former administration with Farmer-Labor loyalists.[144]

The strike of 1934 had been brewing for a while. This was a time of labor upheaval all over the United States, and in Minneapolis, the Citizens' Alliance (CA), a protofascist cabal of business owners, was making life hell for laborers. Tensions erupted with the Teamsters in May; the CA made hay out of the fact that a few of the strike leaders were Communists. They worked themselves—and as much of white-collar Minneapolis as they could persuade—into a lather over supposed Communist infiltration. In the framing of the CA, this wasn't just a battle to continue to exploit workers during an economic depression; it was also a fight for the soul of American society.[145] Governor Olson, a labor sympathizer, was closely following events. The strike began on May 16; on May 19, city and private police beat up strikers for maintaining a picket line. Violence escalated throughout the month—but only because the workers weren't going to take this sitting down, and they fought back.

Minneapolis city officials requested that Olson send out the National Guard. He mobilized but did not deploy them. Olson had been serving as a mediator, and he had faith that a peaceful resolution could be reached. He succeeded by the end of the month.

If Olson thought he had some breathing room to recover, he was mistaken. Between the strike itself and some high drama that was coming his way from Liggett, he was about to have a tumultuous summer.

Labor leader Frank Ellis would later tell a story about going to see Olson in his office at the state capitol one day "around August" and running into Liggett in the reception room. The two of them went in together to meet Olson.[146]

The governor rose from his chair and greeted them, asking them what their business was.

"Well, I will be brief, Floyd," said Liggett. "I don't know what Frank's business is, but there is no secrets [*sic*] about mine." He told Olson how the *Mid-West American* was losing business and he himself was losing money on it. He assured Olson that he supported the Farmer-Labor Party, as well as Olson. He would appreciate more business from the State of Minnesota for his paper. Olson replied that he already gave Liggett as much business as he could afford. Liggett reminded him that there was a Wisconsin newspaper that also got funds from Minnesota, courtesy of Olson.

"Well, however, Liggett, you want to remember that I am ambitious. I want to go places, and it is necessary for me to take care of the papers out of the State as well as in the State."

"Well, I will tell you, Governor, I have used that paper very effectively for you and the Farmer Labor Party, but I can use it just as effectively against you."

Olson, angered, rose from his seat and banged his fist on his desk. "You can take your damned paper and use it any way you see fit, and now get the hell out of here."

This anecdote captures the personalities of these two men, but sources conflict surrounding the end of Olson and Liggett's working relationship. Assuming that this incident did happen, it must have occurred months earlier than when Ellis said it did, no later than early June. In addition, perusal of some correspondence from the governor's office suggests a more gradual separation. At any rate, Liggett not only resigned in late June 1934 but also published a pamphlet justifying himself, *Why I Resigned as Editor of the Austin American*. He aired petty workplace grievances in a tone that implied scandal.

Over in Minneapolis, the employers did not keep up their end of the bargain, and the strike resumed in July. This time, the Teamsters had the backing of all unions, and the Citizens Alliance faced a general strike. In the riots that followed, men died on the side of the laborers striking for better wages and working conditions and on the side of the petit-bourgeois Minneapolitans who had been manipulated by Citizens Alliance propaganda into taking up arms against the laborers. On July 26, Governor Olson declared martial law in Minneapolis and mobilized four thousand national guardsmen to protect the strikers. This backfired for him politically, as he faced allegations of authoritarianism. The strikers were also disgruntled by the pro-employer prejudices of the military command, who took actions that undermined the strike.

In August, Olson was still in the thick of the strike. Liggett was demanding immediate reimbursement that he felt he was owed, and Olson's private secretary, Vince A. Day, tried to handle it. On August 2, Day wrote to the journalist,

> *Dear Walter,*
>
> *Your letter was not answered earlier for the reason, as you are undoubtedly aware, we have been and now are engaged with the strike situation in Minneapolis.*
>
> *I am submitting your statement of account to the Board of Directors of the Austin American...with the recommendation that they pay the claim. I trust that they will do so.*[147]

The board did not follow up quickly enough for Liggett's satisfaction, and soon, Day received a letter from Liggett written on his official *Mid-West American* stationery, which he was keeping for himself, informing Day that he was taking legal action. "I am enclosing the summons and complaint. Will you accept service in the Governor's name and return the acknowledgement to me?…I hope that undue publicity can be avoided….However, this is not my fault."[148]

On August 21, both sides in the strike reached an agreement, but Olson had no such luck with Liggett, whose behavior toward him continued in a bombastic vein.[149] Liggett did not stop even when the legal issues regarding the *Austin American* were finally resolved. The *Mid-West American* denounced Olson in every single issue. This was not the only topic it covered, but it was Walter's pet cause, and in December, the Liggetts moved to Minneapolis, Olson's old stomping grounds, to dig up dirt on him. They investigated his mob connections and corruption in Minneapolis more broadly. That was how they learned about Isadore.

In the autumn of 1935, "rival liquor dealers" would tell the FBI that "the group [headed by Barney Berman, Isadore and Brownstein] operates two liquor stores…besides having an interest in at least three liquor cafes, the Keystone Bar, Powers, and the Six-Twenty Club [usually written '620 Club']."[150]

Because Isadore was a convicted felon, he could not obtain a liquor license. However, he transitioned into becoming a shadow operator of numerous liquor stores and establishments like bars, hotels and restaurants that served alcohol. The mob's (not just Isadore's) long-standing ties to corrupt law enforcement had blossomed into a complex system of kickbacks, tip-offs and staged raids, reaching into gambling dens, brothels and the back rooms of seemingly legitimate businesses. Hitmen advertised their services in the right restaurants. In barbershops, crews planned their next break-in. They were shameless and operated almost in the open, almost with impunity. In addition to the police, gangsters spent money on politicians. The Feds believed that "[the Combination] supported an outsider in the Mayor's race campaign [in 1933], and, at the last moment, switched to the party which ultimately elected its candidate. In return, the gang was given practical control of the city."[151]

Around this time, or soon after, Isadore began to call himself "Mr. Ferguson." Later, he would take to introducing himself as "Dr. Ferguson." Sid Hartman, the sports journalist who died in 2020 after a century of life that spanned Prohibition and COVID-19, wrote in his memoir that Isadore's "friends called him Fergie" and it was the "newspapers and the cops [who] always referred to him as Kid Cann."[152]

The Liggetts had some difficulty getting people to give them information exposing Olson's collusion with the underworld. Part of the reluctance was caused by fear, but some of it may also have been gratitude to mobsters who had helped them in some way. The journalist Eddie Schwartz, who knew Isadore from their youth, had a rosy view of Isadore's machinations with liquor licenses.

> [Isadore] *took care of his family and his friends—putting them in business—which is the old reliable U.S. way. He just saw to it that they were in business.*
>
> *We were just coming out of a severe depression. When the liquor business came back, people were broke and it was hard to go into business, especially the liquor business.*[153]

There were some Minneapolis residents who helped the Liggetts. Their daughter wrote, "Men and women…brought [them] the evidence they needed. A police official's wife used to meet them secretly in the middle of the night. Twice someone brushed by Edith on the street and slipped her pieces of paper containing information on the state pardon racket"—that is, allegations that Governor Olson was selling pardons in return for political favors or donations.[154] One of Olson's supporters, at the suggestion of Vince A. Day, wrote a hit piece on Walter Liggett, accusing him of singling out Olson for abuse and of being in the pocket of Republican Senator Thomas D. Schall, a longtime friend of Liggett's.

The Liggetts sent the children to Wisconsin for the summer, visiting them on weekends. To save money, they moved from Harriet Avenue to a dilapidated Portland Avenue house rented out by Senator Schall. It was there that, on the evening of Sunday, June 23, 1935, a policeman came to the door. He told Liggett that Ed Goff, the Hennepin County attorney and a friend of Floyd Olson's, had charged him with abduction of two minor children. The charge was so outlandish that Liggett asked the policeman, in jest, "if he didn't also have a warrant for bank robbery."[155]

Liggett moved for a change of venue for his case, from Minneapolis to St. Paul. Though the cities were adjacent, there was sufficient difference between them to make the move worthwhile. If nothing else, the racketeers there were more dependent on politicians in St. Paul than in Minneapolis. The judge granted his motion, over the prosecution's objection. It was a

Congressman Thomas D. Schall and his sons, 1917. *Courtesy of Hennepin County Library.*

piece of rare good fortune in what would prove to be a life-ruining court case. The charges expanded as time wore on. By the time Liggett went to trial, the testimonial evidence against him had grown so outrageous that the judge suggested to the jury that the prosecution's witnesses had perjured themselves.

There can be no doubt that the prosecution was politically motivated. Ed Goff was "very anxious" in late June to meet with Olson, and "I believe," said Day, "that it is in connection with the arrest of Liggett."[156] The county attorney requested another meeting months later to discuss the trial.[157] It was a matter that should not have concerned Olson at all, if it merely involved the sexual assault of a teenager.

Walter Liggett's reputation was ruined. His powerful friends around the country abandoned him. The court costs knocked the family sideways, and the *Mid-West American* was hemorrhaging money. His wife's mail arrived already opened. Break-ins became frequent at their home.[158] And yet the Liggetts kept up their reporting on crime and corruption.

Edith Liggett had to be the one to draft the story of the eventful night of October 24, which came out in the October 30 issue of the *Mid-West American*. Her husband was out of commission for the time being. Mrs. Liggett told her readers,

> *Liggett had a tooth kicked out, both eyes blackened, one ear nearly torn off, and suffered many contusions about the face and head besides being severely bruised by kicks in the abdomen, ribs and chest. For a time it was feared that he had several ribs broken. He was taken to Swedish hospital soon after the beating where he remained for two days. He is still confined at home under the doctor's care.*

It all started when Annette Fawcett, an ex-wife of magazine editor Billy Fawcett of *Captain Billy's Whiz Bang* fame, invited Walter Liggett to come to her hotel room. She was a fashionable woman well known for her gatherings of the Minnesota elite and was said to be a mistress, or former mistress, of Governor Olson. On Wednesday, October 23, Fawcett telephoned the office of the *Mid-West American* "several times and asked for my husband, saying the call was important." She left a number, and Liggett called her back. "Mrs. Fawcett told him she had some very vital information concerning his pending trial on frame-up charges brought by the Olson gang." They made plans to meet on Friday night. The next day, Liggett received a letter from Fawcett that she'd sent two days earlier, asking him to call her. Remembering that he had an engagement on Friday night, Edith suggested that he call Fawcett again. Fawcett told him to "come down to the Radisson right away." Liggett asked his wife to come with him, but she had a headache and declined.

Annette Fawcett and her husband, Billy Fawcett, 1923. *Courtesy of Hennepin County Library.*

Soon after my husband arrived at Mrs. Fawcett's apartment she received a telephone call. He heard her say "The gentleman is here now." She then turned to him, said that Kid Cann was on the phone, and asked my husband if he wanted to talk to him. My husband replied that he had nothing to say to Kid Cann then or at any other time.

Mrs. Fawcett sent out for a bottle of liquor and suggested to my husband that he should hire an attorney in his pending trial instead of conducting the case himself. He admitted that he would prefer having an attorney, but said that the first firm he had consulted had asked for

> *$1,500 fees. Mrs. Fawcett then intimated that she could get him counsel for nothing. She named a firm of attorneys and my husband told her that…he would not accept them if they would take his case for nothing. Mrs. Fawcett expressed great sympathy with my husband and said she knew it was a frame-up.*

More people joined them in the room, and Liggett socialized with them. Around eleven o'clock, "Kid Cann suddenly made his appearance. He was introduced. It was the first time my husband had ever seen him." When the man with whom Liggett had mostly been speaking left for the night,

> *Kid Cann immediately began asking my husband why he was attacking him in the Mid-West American. My husband told him it was nothing personal, but he was tired of seeing a gang of underworld crooks run the city of Minneapolis and that he intended to expose Floyd Olson's connections with the vice syndicates.*
>
> *Kid Cann then suggested that if the Mid-West American would "lay off" in its attacks on "The Syndicate"* [referring to his own network] *that my husband would "be taken care of." My husband merely laughed and told Kid Cann he did not accept bribes and that if he did take money from racketeers he would be worse than the racketeers. He bluntly told the former bootlegger that while there was nothing personal about it, he intended to continue his attacks.*
>
> *One word* [led] *to another and Kid Cann, without a word of warning suddenly tried to strike my husband while he was sitting in a chair. Mr. Liggett avoided the blow merely by shifting his head, grabbed Kid Cann by the elbows and sat him back in his own chair without any undue violence. My husband weighs 250 pounds and Kid Cann hardly scales 160. My husband also is a trained boxer. He did not wish to create a disturbance in Mrs. Fawcett's apartment and he was so contemptuous of Kid Cann physically that he did not attempt to chastize* [sic] *him for this treacherous and unprovoked attack.*
>
> *Soon after this my husband announced his intention of leaving. Kid Cann, who in the meantime had apologized for his loss of temper, volunteered to drive him home. Very foolishly my husband accepted the offer. Felix Doran accompanied them.*
>
> *As they were driving out Hennepin avenue, Kid Cann suggested that they have one last drink and "forget all hard feelings." Once more my husband, who carries good nature and trust in others to a fault, foolishly agreed.*

Kid Cann, Felix Doran and my husband entered a night club at Eleventh and Hennepin. Kid Cann appeared to know quite a few persons present. He went over to a table where "Brownie" [Brownstein] *was sitting with two girls. Introductions were made all around.*

[Brownstein] *immediately repeated Kid Cann's formula and asked my husband why he was attacking "The Syndicate." My husband again explained that there was nothing personal, but that it was a fight for political decency and he did not expect Cann or* [Brownstein] *to understand or agree with his motives. In the meantime, my husband danced twice with one of the girls.*

[Brownstein], *using almost the same words previously used by Cann, said that if my husband would "lay off" he "would be taken care of." My husband again told him that if he took money under such circumstances he would be a blackmailer and an extortionist. He flatly told both men that there was no purpose gained in making such offers and that he intended to continue his campaign against Floyd Olson and his racketeering friends in the Minneapolis underworld.*

Kid Cann suddenly struck my husband a heavy blow in the mouth when he was talking to [Brownstein]. [Brownstein] *immediately joined in the attack. Several other men also sprang upon him. Although badly punished, my husband regained his feet after being knocked down, and was defending himself. The proprietor and several waiters interfered.*

Realizing that he was hopelessly outnumbered, my husband readily assented when the proprietor asked him to go outside.

As soon as he appeared on the sidewalk a group of several men swarmed out of the café. They cried:

"It's Liggett—the fellow who is giving us all the heat. Let's beat him up."

Others cried: "Come on! Let's give him the works."

My husband tried to enter a taxi-cab parked at the curb, but when members of the gang shouted warnings the driver refused to open the door. He tried to climb into another passing cab with the same results. Then at least seven men assailed him simultaneously.

Mr. Liggett backed into a doorway and defended himself as best he could. His bruised knuckles show that he landed at last two or three heavy blows. He was keeping his feet and beating off successive attackers when a heavyset man ran up crying:

"I am your friend, Liggett, Come on! We'll clean up these [sons of bitches].*" My husband thought some chivalrous stranger had come to his aid. He turned to meet a man who was hitting at him from behind and when*

he did so his pretended rescuer struck him a heavy blow which knocked him to the pavement. Whereupon the entire gang started kicking at his prostrate body. They jumped on his chest and repeatedly kicked at his groin. He was mercilessly kicked about the head and face. In a few seconds he received a beating that would have killed many a man with less strength and vitality.

A crowd collected and my husband thinks a policeman came—although he must have stayed on the outskirts of the crowd. My husband regained his feet and staggered into a taxicab. The driver brought him home. I immediately telephoned three times for an ambulance, but there was a delay in its arrival of nearly two hours because the only one available seemed on another call. When the ambulance finally arrived my husband was taken to Swedish hospital.

When two detectives first came to the hospital, they took my husband's statement and then asked him if he would sign a complaint. He said he would. They promised to return later.

Apparently, after these two detectives, who seemed honest and sympathetic, reached police headquarters, they were instructed that nothing was to be done about the assault except to white-wash the perpetrators. They did not return to the hospital Friday with the complaint.

I called up police headquarters and finally arranged…an interview with [the] *captain of detectives. He was sneering and unsympathetic. He claimed that investigation had proved the affair to be a drunken brawl and that my husband was the aggressor. Later the two gangsters* [Isadore and Brownstein] *gave out a story, concocted with the help of Mrs. Fawcett and her secretary which alleged that my husband had solicited a bribe, that he had repeatedly attacked Kid Cann in Mrs. Fawcett's apartment; that my husband was drunk; and that in the café he was abusive and provoked an attack. Cann and* [Brownstein] *denied all knowledge of the attack made on my husband outside in the street. The police—who for years have protected "The Syndicate" gang and certain powerful gamblers closely connected with them—flatly refused to issue a complaint for assault and battery, and sneeringly suggested that my husband might be arrested for attacking* [Brownstein] *who was said to have had his thumb broken in the melee.*

The falsity of the charges that my husband was drunk are best refuted by the hospital records which distinctly state that while liquor was on his breath he showed no symptoms whatever of intoxication. Several nurses and internes [sic] *can verify the report of the examining physician.*[159]

Neither Liggett nor Isadore was exactly Emily Post. It is not outside the realm of possibility that Liggett verbally provoked Isadore and Brownstein, if nothing else. Liggett certainly had a motive to tell his wife that he had done nothing to trigger the violence against him. But of course, Isadore and Brownstein were their own masters, and nobody forced them or their associates to attack Liggett. They did that willingly.

In the issue in which Edith reported the beating of her husband, the *Mid-West American* carried a story headlined, "Council Breaks Laws to Favor Syndicate Gang: Farmer-Labor Machine Gives Ex-Bootleggers Monopoly in Booze Trade." The article alleged that the Minneapolis City Council "displayed rank favoratism [*sic*]" in issuing liquor licenses to Tommy Banks's and Isadore's gangs. Edith Liggett wrote defiantly, "I do not believe that the weird yarn [about her husband soliciting a bribe] told by the ex-bootlegger Kid Cann and his confederates will fool anyone." She was wrong. The press had a field day at Walter's expense, repeating the same tale that the captain of detectives had thrown at Edith. Walter Liggett was now jeered at in print as a brawler, a drunk, a hypocrite, a crooked liar. He developed pleurisy as a result of his injuries and was bedridden until his trial started in early November.[160]

Edith Liggett sent the ACLU a plea for support in Walter's case and enclosed a report on Isadore. The information contained in it shows how uneven the quality of their sources were:

> *Kid Cann*['s] *real name is Bloomfield. Under the name of Bloomfield, in pre-prohibition days he was picked up several times for picking pockets, and then, when he was about 18 or 19, became a pimp with four Jewish girls out on the street working for him….*
>
> *About six years ago he killed Charley Goldberg, a businessman, coming out of a cafe on Nicollet between 3RD and 4TH streets. He had picked a fight with Goldberg earlier in the evening. At the funeral Rabbi Minda spoke of the shame to the Jewish people such men as Cann are.*
>
> *During 1929–1930–1931–1932 Kid Cann spent most of his time in New Orleans smuggling alcohol and other liquors from the West Indies for the Minneapolis bootleg Syndicate. While there he was in a shooting affray in which a man was killed.*
>
> *When Verne Miller was booked as Public Enemy No. 5 of the entire United States, Kid Cann was with him in a cafe on 6th Ave. N. in the colored district. Police burst into the cafe to capture Miller, and Kid Cann helped him shoot his way out….*

> *Kid Cann, Brownie Bronstein* [sic], *Barney Berman and Meyer Schuldberg are at present leaders in the liquor Syndicate—a gang of ex-bootleggers to whom the Olson machinery is trying to give a complete liquor monopoly in the Twin Cities. All of them have prison records and most of them are now under indictment on one count or another. Kid Cann has an indictment standing against him in North Dakota....*
>
> *Kid Cann and some of his buddies were having a wild party at the Dykman* [sic] *hotel. A hotel detective protested—very politely, since he was afraid of Cann. Cann hit him over the head with a chair and then kicked him when he fell to the floor.*
>
> *Kid Cann boasts that he has shot seven men, but the general report is that the real number is three—killed two and crippled one.*[161]

On Saturday, November 9, the jury found Walter Liggett not guilty. Judge Enerson assessed all the trial costs against Hennepin County. Walter and Edith Liggett celebrated with local friends, while government officials spied on them, and Walter declared his intentions to request a grand jury investigation.

The Liggetts were "almost giddy with relief" after the verdict, but their lives were still hard.[162] They were mired in debt. Edith Liggett, who alone had supported the family during her husband's convalescence from the assault and pleurisy, had resorted to begging their friends and colleagues for money. The Liggetts now lived in an apartment at 1825 Stevens Avenue South instead of renting a house.

Walter Liggett "was in a relaxed and smiling mood" shortly before five o'clock on December 9, when he picked up ten-year-old Marda from the Lake Street public library, her after-school refuge. Marda, a future librarian, conscientiously put away *The Green Fairy Book* on the shelf. "Bundle up," her father said, "shivering dramatically to make [her] smile."

They next picked up Edith Liggett and a friend at the printing plant, went to the grocery store, dropped off the friend at his bus stop, bought a copy of the *New York Times* and headed home. As they pulled into the alley of their apartment building, Marda saw the full moon in the navy-blue sky. The snow had stopped falling, but white powder dusted the parked cars, clearly illuminated by the light from windows flanking the alley. Marda could see the lights on in her family's second-floor apartment, where twelve-year-old Wallace was listening to *Jack Armstrong: The All-American Boy*, a children's radio serial. Walter Liggett parked on the left side, right below the windows of their apartment. A dark car entered the alley and drove toward the Liggetts.

The curb was too high to open the driver's side door, so Walter slid across the front seat and got out on the passenger side. He opened the door to the back seat and teased Marda, telling her he would bring in the newspaper and she could get the heavy box of groceries. It was only then that Walter seemed to notice the other car. He gestured to Marda and her mother to wait in the car, smiled at them and then moved over to the front fender to let the other car go by. Marda saw a hand holding a gun in the window of the dark car and ducked. She heard gunfire, and when it had stopped, she looked up. Her mother was getting out of the car. Her father lay on the ground.

Wallace was looking out the window in alarm when his sister burst into the apartment. "Daddy's been shot!" she said. Neighbors, cops and reporters surged into the alley. Edith could not give up hope that her husband would live, in spite of the bullets embedded around his heart. As he lay next to the car, she rested his head in her lap. He was still warm to her touch. She stayed outside with him, in the alley, in a tableau of grief on display for the fast-arriving newsmen and their flashbulbs.[163]

Plainclothesman Fred Higgins was on patrol with his partner, Fred Schroeder, near Fifth and Cedar when the call came in from dispatch. Higgins was behind the wheel, and by his own account, he drove as fast as he could. "Schroeder warned me to slow down, and I went like hell." In the alley, they found a crowd already gathered. Higgins went into the building to speak with Edith Liggett, who by that time had gone into her apartment.

"I recognized Kid Cann's face," she said. "He was the one that had a grin on his face!"

"How do you know it's Kid Cann?" asked Higgins. "Do you know Kid Cann?"

"Yes, I have never met him, but he has been pointed out to me several times." Edith Liggett was adamant. "I would never forget his face."

"What complexion has Kid Cann got?" Higgins asked her.

"He has the same complexion that I have. I got a good look at him and he had a grin on his face."[164]

Isadore was picked up by the police and brought in to the station. Captain Marxen conducted an interview.

"What is your full name?"

"Isadore Blumenfield."

"Where do you live?"

"1525 Plymouth North." That was his mother's address, not his own.

"Are you married?"

"Yes." He was not.

"How old are you?"

"Thirty-four years." He was thirty-five years old.

"Have you a family?"

"There are no children."

"What is your business?"

"Sales manager for Chesapeake Brands."

Marxen proceeded to walk Isadore through his movements that day, leading up to an alibi. At 4:30 p.m., said Isadore, he went to his office at 115 Fifth Street Northeast and stayed there

> *until about 5:05 to be exact because I wanted to make the barber shop on time….I did not have my car today. My brother had it. I was using Meyer* [Schuldberg's] *car all day, a Dodge Sedan. Meyer went down and got the boy in the shipping room to drive me downtown and this boy took me downtown in…a Chevrolet Coupe. As he drove me away, I took my heater with me. We stopped off at the St. Anthony Motor and I talked to Mr. Ewes, the owner, and asked him if this heater would work. This must have been about 5:15 PM at the latest. Ewes said wait until we ask the foreman. The foreman was called and I was told to put on another thermostat. I said alright, I will bring my car in tomorrow. I was there until about 5:30 PM asking him about window glasses and radiator fluid. The boy was waiting for me and took me to the Liquor Mart at #12 South 5th Street. I walked in there and met Lou Galinson. I said to Lou, I am going over and get a shave. He said wait and I will walk up to the corner with you. When we got on the corner, there was a coal company there and the wind was blowing so hard he asked me to step into the doorway and we talked there for two or three minutes and I went right over to the barber shop, the Artistic Barber Shop on Hennepin between 5th and 6th St. Garfinkle is the proprietor. I had a shave, my spats cleaned, shoes shined and a tonic.*

"Who was the barber you had?

"I always have the barber in the middle. His first name is Ted. The colored boy shined my shoes."

"What time was this?"

"I was in the barber shop from about 5:45 p.m. until 6:30 p.m. The manicurist was there and a girl who is a friend of the manicurist."

"Mr. Blumenfield, do you know Walter Liggett, the deceased?"

"Yes."

"How long have you known him?" asked Marxen.

"I met him once."

"Where was that meeting?"

"At the Radisson Hotel, room 1013."

"Was that by appointment or a chance meeting?"

"It was a chance meeting. Mrs. Fawcett called me and told me that Liggett was there. She told me to come up, and I did."

"Did you have an argument at that time at the Radisson?"

"He argued with me," said Isadore. "He was drunk."

"What was the argument about?"

> *I walked in there and he was drunk with his feet on another chair and he said to me, "So you are Kid Cann." He got to asking me if I was a good friend of Floyd Olson. I said no, I know him but have never had the pleasure of talking to him. He then asked if I knew Ed. Goff, I said No. He then called me a liar and many other names, so I told him not to be talking that way and that I did not come up to argue with him; that I was there to ask him why he should write those things against me as I was on the other side of the fence now, on the legit, and wanted to be let alone. He said "You are one of those smart Jews" and he got up and made a pass at me* [meaning "took a swing at me"] *in the apartment. I pushed him and he fell over and broke the leg of a chair. I finally got him to keep quiet and he started to proposition me about a trial he had coming up and that he needed a lawyer and had no money. I asked him what has that got to do with me. Well he said before I am through with you I will have you sleeping in the same bed with Floyd. I asked him what he wanted to do that for as I did not know him (Liggett). He said "I have got trouble and have to take care of myself." He finally asked me for $1500 if he would lay off of me. So I said to him that I would not give anything as I had not done anything wrong to give him anything. He was sitting around there until about 12 or 12:30 at night. He finally asked me to take him home. I did not want to but he insisted on it, so I agreed to take him home and we walked down to 5th Street where my car was parked. Another fellow by the name of Dorn was with us and he got in the car with us also.*
>
> *Liggett said let's stop and get a drink. I said no, you better go home, but he insisted on getting a drink and we stopped off at the Tia Juana and had a drink, and he disappeared and walked outside and that is the last I saw of him until I understood he got slugged outside. This is the last I saw or heard of him until I heard of his being shot.*

At the end of the interview, Marxen asked, "Is this a true statement of facts to the best of your knowledge?"

"Absolutely true 100 percent."[165]

Isadore had been treated gently by the police, who were very accommodating throughout the arrest process, but now he was jailed. On the morning of December 11, he was brought to the showup room at the jail (where the police presented what we now call lineup) with seven or eight other men. Edith Liggett, her lawyer and her brother-in-law came into the room. Supervisor of Detectives John Hilborn asked Edith "if anyone in that crowd did the shooting." She replied that it was "the man in the center and pointed directly to Kid Cann."

Isadore exclaimed, "Yes, you have seen my pictures in the papers."[166]

Edith Liggett was not the only witness who said that the shooter was Isadore. A neighbor, Wesley J. Andersch, who had served time in the workhouse at the same time as Isadore, came forward. But Andersch was not a reliable witness. He had a history of erratic behavior, and his wife sought a divorce on the basis of physical cruelty and extreme dishonesty, which Vince A. Day, now a municipal judge, granted.[167]

Some years after the murder, a government official received information about the shooting that he considered credible. A carpenter named Fritz Danielson told him he had witnessed the Liggett murder but did not come forward at the time. Isadore and Schuldberg threatened Danielson and ordered him to leave town but promised him money to move. He did move out of state, but when he wrote to Isadore to ask for the money, the letter was given to postal service investigators, and Danielson was charged with extortion. He received a suspended two-year sentence and was on probation for five years.[168]

Edith Liggett had no confidence that Isadore would be convicted.[169] She believed that Olson had ordered the hit, and she would eventually testify to that belief at trial. She continued to oppose Olson for his corruption and ties to the underworld. But Vince A. Day's February 10, 1936 memorandum to Olson suggests that Olson did not fight his enemies with physical violence. "Nothing is to be gained by swinging your Viking ax against such worms as…Mrs. Liggett. You merely dignify them, and increase their audience by your *replies* to their attacks" (emphasis mine). Day noted, "It is important that some offensive be taken to silence the many wild rumors concerning your connections with the underworld," but the offensive he recommended was to arrange "an investigation to

Isadore (*center*) and friends. This photo may have been taken in the wake of his acquittal for the murder of Walter Liggett. *Minnesota Historical Society.*

disprove it....Maybe it would be sufficient to send an investigator out here for the purpose of finding out the truth."[170]

Dave Garfinkle, owner of the Artistic Barbershop, backed up Isadore's alibi, as did his employees, although the times they recalled him being there varied by as much as twenty minutes.

Isadore was acquitted.

"Those in the know," wrote George MacKinnon to journalist Fred Friendly decades after the trial, "generally considered that Kid Cann had killed Liggett. However, knowing Cann, I think it would have been more likely that he hired somebody to do it."[171] One theory, to which MacKinnon gave some weight, holds that the hit man may have, coincidentally, resembled Isadore. Another theory I have heard is that Isadore, while not the shooter, was a passenger in the car, which at least would explain why he did not have a better alibi.

"Rumor has it," said MacKinnon, "that the barber that supplied the alibi was kept on Cann's payroll for the rest of his natural life."[172]

Governor Harold E. Stassen. *Library of Congress Prints and Photographs Division.*

Stories abound of bribes promised by Isadore and company in this case, some of them impossible, contradictory or unlikely. Some of them are believable.[173] That aside, we cannot blame the alibi barber, who was motivated by more than venality.

Around seven o'clock in the evening on November 15, 1935, Dave Garfinkle arrived home at 536 Logan Avenue North. He parked and got out of the car. As he reached the door of his house, a car passed. He heard a crash and looked closely, trying to get a license plate number, but the car's lights were off. It was a dark sedan. Garfinkle watched as it turned west onto Sixth Avenue North. He had received threatening phone calls recently, and now he took no chances. He called the police, and a pair of investigators, Colston and Mealey, came to his house.

They looked in Garfinkle's car and saw that there was a rock with a note on the front seat:

> *This warning is no joke the same as those phone calls*
> *We again warn you*
> *Dont talk*
> *Tell those in your shop not to talk*
> *We know where they live.*[174]

Floyd B. Olson's health failed. He died of cancer soon after the murder trial. The *St. Paul Daily News* reported in August 1936, "Floyd Olson died on the threshold to greater things. A seat in the United States Senate was just a step away. The Presidency of the United States was a possibility."[175] In a few years, the Farmer-Labor Party began to collapse. When the Republican Harold E. Stassen ran for governor against the incumbent Farmer-Labor member Elmer Benson, he played on voters' antisemitism by drawing their attention to the presence of high-ranking Jews in the Farmer-Labor Party and won.[176]

The Death of a Third Newsman

In November 1936, scandal sheet editor Arthur Kasherman approached the FBI with information about rackets in Minneapolis, especially Ed Morgan's, "but," wrote the special agent in charge, he "was unable to give anything specific, and it appeared that the purpose that Kasherman had in his own mind was in order to stir up as much trouble as possible."[177]

In 1937, Kasherman was prosecuted for extorting twenty-five dollars from a brothel owner to refrain from writing about her establishment. The trial was a disaster for Kasherman. One of its most dramatic elements was testimony from Hyman Peyser, a relative by marriage of Isadore's brother Harry. Peyser testified that Kasherman had tried to extort him on a previous occasion. When Peyser finished speaking, Kasherman shouted at him, "You were willing to pay me to retain me in the Kid Cann murder case!" The *Tribune* noted in its reporting that "Peyser did not figure in the investigation of the Walter Liggett slaying or in Kid Cann's subsequent trial for it." The judge had Kasherman's outburst stricken from the court record.

As the defense counsel was examining another witness, Kasherman exploded, "I don't want him as an attorney!" Judge Selover ordered Kasherman to be quiet: "We're trying to protect you from yourself."[178] Before long, Kasherman was representing himself in court—badly. He was sentenced to up to five years in Stillwater. He would be absent from the city during a shift in the balance of underworld power.

The gambler Chickie Berman had been in Minneapolis for a few years, and now his brother, Davie, joined him, shortly after getting out of Sing Sing. According to Davie's daughter, writer Susan Berman, powerful New York mob bosses had wanted to reward Davie for refusing to snitch, and he asked for permission take over the corner of the gambling business that they held in Minneapolis.[179] That was why Davie was there in 1938 when New York Judge Nathan David Perlman called, says mob chronicler Michael Benson. Perlman was arranging for Jewish gangsters to beat up Nazi sympathizers all over the country. Given Isadore's unsavory reputation, Perlman did not want to contact him, so he reached out to Davie instead. Davie agreed.[180] Assuming this conversation did happen, Davie would not have needed much persuading. Using his fists on antisemites had been a childhood hobby of his.[181] In Benson's telling, after Davie finished the call with Perlman, he called Isadore and asked him if he wanted to join in. Isadore said yes.[182] However, neither I nor local mob expert Paul Maccabee have seen evidence that Davie and Isadore ever worked together.

Davie made plans to disrupt a gathering of the Silver Shirts, a Nazi sympathizer group making inroads in Minneapolis. "Be at the office at seven p.m. and bring anybody and anything you've got," he told his cohorts. As if there were any doubt about what he meant by "anything you've got," Davie "put on a pair of brass knuckles and distributed clubs."

In a grim parade of Cadillacs, they drove to the Elks Lodge and sent in a lookout. According to Susan, "As soon as the head of the Silver Shirts got on the podium and started yelling for an end to 'all the Jew bastards in this city,' the lookout signaled to my father."

What happened next would go down in the annals of Minneapolis Nazi-beating history.

> *Davie led the group in his pin-striped suit. He mounted the stage and grabbed the burly leader, yelling, "Nobody says that about Jews." He bashed* [the speaker] *on the head with his club. His men swung onto the stage, beating up every Silver Shirt they could, and the audience started screaming and running out. Davie tore down the picture of Hitler and the swastikas and ripped them to shreds. He had to be pulled off the leader of the Silver Shirts; his men feared he'd kill him. The meeting had turned into a total stampede by this time with everyone who could still walk running to the door.*
>
> *The whole attack took ten minutes. At the end, my father, his suit completely bloodied, took to the podium and said into the microphone in a cold controlled voice, "This is a warning. Anybody who says anything against the Jews gets the same treatment. Only next time it will be worse." He then took out a pistol and fired a shot into the air. At that he and his men left the hall, got into the cars, and drove back to the Office. It took two more such "warnings" to make his point.*[183]

When the Silver Shirts assembled at the Ark Masonic Lodge, Isadore and his men showed up, armed with machine guns. A "prominent" member of the Jewish community who was also in attendance told Isadore to leave without violence or else "all the Jews in Minneapolis [will] be killed as a reprisal." Isadore allowed himself to be persuaded, and no one was harmed.[184]

Susan writes proudly that Davie was seen as a "good racketeer," in contrast to what the city regarded as a bad one in Isadore. "My father's group was known to be the more aboveboard and legitimate of the two factions."[185]

The antipathy to Isadore must have been widespread, because the FBI heard that "Cann is reported to be the most hated Jew in Minneapolis because he has secured for himself too much power in the liquor business.

Furthermore, "He is reported to secure his power through connections with the various Minneapolis City Aldermen. It is reported that he has control of twenty-four of the twenty-six aldermen."[186]

But there were more camps than the Combination and the Davie/Chickie Bermans. Ed Morgan's Syndicate, as far as the FBI could determine in 1939, controlled the vice rackets in Minneapolis.[187] And yet Morgan was not singled out by the Feds as the "most hated Irishman in Minneapolis."

On July 7, 1941, Marvin Kline, an electrical engineer who had served as city council president, started his term as mayor of Minneapolis. During his campaign, he had pledged to shut down the rackets. Ten days later, the FBI was told that Davie and Chickie "made arrangements to take over control of gambling and vice in Minneapolis through their being able to control the Minneapolis City Council with the incoming administration of Marvin Kline."[188]

Davie and Chickie may have had a big slice of the pie, but the other vice operators were still in business. Kasherman, who had been released from prison in September 1940, had no shortage of material and no shortage of enemies. The day after Christmas 1942, two men with blackjacks beat him outside a drug store "at Sixteenth and Nicollet. He was taken to General hospital with scalp wounds." The *Pioneer Press* reported that this was the fourth time he had been attacked in his career as a newsman.[189]

In 1943, the FBI field office in St. Paul published a report on "vice conditions" in the region. The locally grown gangsters seemed to be ascendant. The report characterized Ed Morgan, still at the Dyckman Hotel, as "chief contact with the police department" and "recognized head of the Syndicate" (a term used here to refer to the community of racketeers). The Feds thought Tommy Banks was still below Morgan but relatively powerful. As for Isadore:

> *Isadore Blumenfeld, alias Kid Cann, has control, along with Tom Banks, of the liquor faction. He exercises his control through the aldermen only. In this manner he is powerful enough to close any place operating without his permission or supervision….*[190]
>
> *If Blumenfeld and his associates do not want* [a particular liquor store or bar] *to open, the same is not permitted to have a license issued for it. Information has been secured from numerous individuals in the past, as reflected in the St. Paul file, to the effect that most of the Minneapolis City Aldermen and the various mayors who have been in office in the past, have completely cooperated with the "Syndicate" in these liquor dealings.*

> *It is known that Blumenfeld and his associates control all of the liquor stores in Minneapolis, either directly owning these stores or getting a large percentage of the profits therefrom.*
>
> *Blumenfeld, at the present time, is regarded as a somewhat high class hoodlum in Minneapolis and a certain degree of respect is had for him by the underworld in general. He has this respect due to the fact that he has connections with the "Syndicate" and has accumulated a sizeable fortune through his illicit liquor dealings.*

The writer added, "In the past [Blumenfeld] was regarded as a 'punk' and was the type of individual who could be used on almost any job by other characters."[191] The following sentence returns to the present: "Blumenfeld can generally be found frequenting the Radisson Hotel where he sometimes gives large parties."[192] In this cold catalog of characteristics, the writer spares no thought for analysis or contemplation of his subject's inner world. Did that "punk" ever dream that someday he would host parties in a hotel? Could he have foreseen, as Prohibition neared, the tide of history on which he would rise? The Isadore of 1943 had come a long way from the Isadore of 1919, and the Feds were finding it difficult to pin down the extent of his influence.

> *Blumenfeld's name, it will be noted, has been connected with various places of vice in Minneapolis. However, information has been secured that various higher-ups open these places and merely use KID CANN's name for publicity purposes in order to give the place a name. It is not believed that he is actually the owner of any of these places but possibly gets out a small cut out of their profits.*[193]

Davie and Chickie Berman are classified in the report as mere "stooges and cogs in the wheel."[194]

On the other hand, the Reverend Harry J. Soltau, who railed against vice in the city of Minneapolis, received a letter a year before the vice report was issued claiming that "[Police] Officer Hart has to take his list of complaints to one Chickie Bierman [*sic*] to find out Who He Can Arrest And Who he Should lay Off Of....This Bierman [*sic*] has This young Hart so tied Up he Cant move." The letter does not even mention Isadore but complains that under Marvin Kline's administration, compared to the previous one, "Things Are Just is [*sic*] Bad if not worse." Kline's chief of police was "right in with all the Jews and makes no attempt at Law

Enforcement." It was signed, "The Honest Members of the Minneapolis Police Dept."[195]

As if the cops of Minneapolis weren't aware of Gentile gangsters like Tommy Banks and Ed Morgan!

Selden Menefee, a representative of the Office of Public Opinion Research of Princeton University, wrote in his 1943 book that he had found "signs of militant anti-Semitism to be almost entirely lacking in the Middle West—except for Minneapolis." One of his sources, a politically liberal professional, told him, "Anti-Semitism is stronger here than anywhere I have ever lived."[196]

Sid Hartman noted in his memoir that "there was anti-Semitism involved" in how Isadore was perceived in Minneapolis.[197] In contrast to that perception, Hartman recalled Isadore and his associates with fondness.

> *My favorite stop* [as a newsboy] *was at Jack Doyle's restaurant…where all the people who were called "racketeers" hung out—Isadore Blumenfeld, Tommy Banks, Chickie Berman. I would walk in with my papers and get a half-buck, maybe a buck, for a paper. I was selling two-cent newspapers and would walk out of there with ten bucks.*[198]

No matter what he heard about his generous customers and the source of their wealth, Hartman stated firmly, "I stayed loyal to those guys." He admitted that Isadore was the "most notorious man in the group." His family "had all the big liquor stores.…They monopolized the liquor business, and that's why they had so many enemies."[199]

It was about more than liquor. Isadore's dealings with the Excelsior Baking Company are but one minor example of the shady activities that he got away with during his lifetime.

In 1940, Excelsior Baking Company was having "labor difficulties." Management wanted to change its contract with the union; the union wasn't having it. Management was put in touch with Isadore. District Judge Joyce would excoriate company leadership in 1949:

> *Without inquiring as to the qualifications or business connections of* [Isadore and a confederate], [Excelsior] *committed itself to pay $13,000 if a satisfactory modification of the union contract was obtained. The unsavory reputation of the individuals with whom* [Excelsior] *proposed to deal was revealed long before a modification of the contract was secured and before any payments were actually made.*

Isadore's bright idea for resolving the conflict between management and labor was "sending a letter to the national president of the union and the posting of several notices designed to advise the driver-salesmen of the precarious position of their employer." His manipulation tactics worked, and within a few months, management had the change to the contract that they wanted. Isadore and his companion first received $7,000 for this small service. The cash was "wrapped in a newspaper which was then delivered to [Isadore's friend] on a Minneapolis street corner." The rest of the money was paid in installments, brought out in cash to Isadore's friend while he waited in his car.

When the contract ended in the fall of 1940 and management once more failed to negotiate a contract that they considered favorable, Isadore and his friend were paid $3,500 to "secure a satisfactory contract with the union."[200] Morally, was there a difference between Isadore and the people who hired him?

Isadore was an exploiter, but it didn't hurt his bottom line. He was doing great business.

Samuel Hynes, a few years younger than Sid Hartman, was more clear-eyed. He and Marda Liggett had gone to the same school. When he was eighteen years old, he knowingly went to one of Isadore's bars.

> *Fats Waller is playing at the Happy Hour up on Nicollet. It's a scary place to go, Kid Cann owns it; he runs the rackets in town, he has people beaten up and killed, my father says he's the one who stuck the machine gun out of the car window and shot Marda Liggett's father. There'll be gangsters in his saloon, and a bouncer. But I go anyway, because Fats Waller's there.*[201]

"Kid Cann would bring in Sophie Tucker, Cab Calloway—entertainers like that—to appear at his club," Hartman reminisced. "Then, after hours, they would close the doors and the real show would begin."[202] Musicians who played at Isadore's clubs tend, as Tela Burt did, to recall him in a positive light, as a good tipper and an encouraging patron who reveled in the performances.[203]

Isadore made little effort to hide his connection to the Flame and the Happy Hour, but he grew cagey when official notice was directed at the truth about the clubs' ownership. On the afternoon of March 13, 1940, he sat for a deposition in the University of Minnesota Law School. The case at hand was a suit for defamation against a New York newspaper regarding its reporting on the Liggett murder case. Isadore's attorney, H.Z. Mendow, objected to almost all the questions and advised Isadore not to answer them. Isadore obeyed. This was their approximate refrain:

Mendow: "I object to the question on the ground that it is incompetent, irrelevant and immaterial, and I advise the witness that he may decline to answer the question on the ground that it would tend to incriminate him."

Isadore: "I decline to answer on advice of counsel on the ground that it would tend to incriminate me."

Among the questions that received this response from them were: "What is your business?" "Did you in the latter part of 1935 know one Walter W. Liggett?" "Have you used the name Kid Cann?" "Did you murder Charles Goldberg in 1924?" "Are you now connected with a night club in Minneapolis known as the Happy Hour?"

At the end of the deposition, Mendow said, "I am advising my client that he may refuse to sign this testimony upon the ground that it might tend to incriminate him." Isadore agreed, "I refuse to sign upon advice of counsel, upon the ground that it might tend to incriminate me."[204]

A few months before the deposition, the local chief U.S. probation officer, Ernest J. Meili, received a related inquiry from James V. Bennett, director of the Bureau of Prisons for the Department of Justice. Meili replied,

> *Occasionally the local newspapers make a lot of noise that the State or Local authorities are going after Kid Cann and his ilk. Sometimes I think that these outbursts of "righteous indignation" are merely the preliminaries to another "shakedown."...Most of the licenses to operate liquor stores are in the names of "dummies." The law does not permit persons convicted of liquor offenses to have licenses, but this is easily circumvented by getting the licenses in the name of a person who works in the store as a clerk or flunky. It is quite possible that* [Barney Berman] *owns the store which he operates though it might be well nigh impossible to prove it. It may also be that Kid Cann owns the store and this might be equally difficult to prove.*[205]

In December 1944, Kasherman published the final issue of his paper. The headline ran, "Kline Administration Most Corrupt in History of the City." Kasherman declared, "City wide open! Racketeers in complete control of city government. Police department used as tool by mobsters!" He told his readers, "During the last mayoralty campaign...Kline went up and down the avenue, and shouted that there will be 'no racketeering' during his administration as mayor of the city of Minneapolis—and that the 'Combination'...will not be allowed to operate while he is mayor of the city"—but that had been a lie.[206]

A few weeks later, Kasherman ran into his friend Pearl Von Wald at Pantages Theater, and he invited her to have chow mein with him. They ate dinner at a café at 1425 Chicago Avenue South. They finished eating shortly after eleven o'clock and then left the restaurant. When they went back outside to Kasherman's car at Fifteenth Street, he had a flat tire. The police would discover that it had been deliberately punctured.

Kasherman and Von Wald got into the car all the same. A sedan turned onto the street from Chicago Avenue and parked. A man in the car fired at Kasherman, shattering the glass in his car window. His face bloodied by the glass, Kasherman dropped down into Von Wald's lap. He pushed her out of the car, his blood staining her coat, and then climbed over her to get out himself. Kasherman ran toward Chicago Avenue, away from the shooter. "Don't shoot," he cried out, "for God's sake, don't shoot," and Von Wald heard him say someone's name, as if he knew the man who shot him, but she could not make it out. The victim was "destroyed by a fusillade of bullets."

The *Minneapolis Star Journal* sneered, "His immunity to the fate that caught up with him...was more or less taken for granted around city hall because no one ever took him seriously."[207]

The murder went unsolved. Lee Welch, reporter with the *Minneapolis Tribune*, gave readers a brief history of gangland murders of journalists on January 28, 1945. "Only Liggett's death resulted in an important arrest, Isadore (Kid Cann) Blumenfeld, a Minneapolis character." Welch did not go so far as to accuse Isadore of Kasherman's murder, but the Kid Cann mythos is a distinct entity from Isadore himself. One Minneapolitan with an interest in local history told me that he knows "for a fact" that Isadore killed Kasherman. It is possible that Isadore ordered the hit, but other people had as much or more motive than he did. Kasherman had been going after Ed Morgan for years.

Chapter 5

PERSUASIVE POWER

Mayor Humphrey Clamps Down

Arthur Kasherman's murder was a disgrace to Mayor Kline's administration, about whom everyone knew Kasherman had told the truth: Kline was shamelessly corrupt. Young upstart outsider Hubert H. Humphrey, fresh off the political victory of merging the Democratic Party with the Farmer-Labor Party, melded ambition, idealism and pragmatism in a blend that perhaps had not been seen in Minnesota since the death of Floyd B. Olson. Humphrey made much of the shooting of Kasherman, and a key part of his campaign was his opposition to the rackets.

It was possible that Kline was not only tied up with Davie and Chickie Berman: the FBI heard in spring of 1945 that

> *the Syndicate, especially Kid Cann, has something on Marvin Kline inasmuch as Mayor Kline sometime ago accepted about $9,000 for issuing a liquor license to a certain individual in Minneapolis and the Syndicate purposely did that so they would have something on the Mayor in case he wanted to clamp down on them.*[208]

The voters chose Humphrey.

Mob histories repeat the dialogues between Isadore/his emissaries and Mayor Humphrey and between the mayor and David Berman/his emissaries. They are invariably entertaining, with the mobsters begging and the mayor huffily refusing to go along with business as usual. Humphrey biographer

Hubert H. Humphrey (official photograph), circa 1965. *Library of Congress Prints and Photographs Division.*

Samuel Freedman believes that these stories are likely apocryphal. Humphrey was shot at shortly after taking office, and although this is generally assumed to have been the work of disgruntled mobsters, Freedman suggests that it was a bigot who was enraged by Humphrey's goal of eliminating discrimination in Minneapolis against Jews and Black people.[209]

Humphrey instructed the chief of police to brutally smash up gambling operations. This hit David Berman where it hurt. While Isadore did still have some gambling operations, the bulk of his fortune was in other rackets. But David, who came home from the war, where he fought in the Canadian army in pursuit of vengeance for Jews killed in Europe, now packed up his family and moved to Las Vegas.

Isadore had wedded the beautiful Lillian Lee, who stood by him throughout the Liggett murder trial while she was his mistress. Lillian came from Missouri and described her family as religious Christians descended, on the father's side, from Robert E. Lee.[210] Before her marriage, Lillian worked as a prostitute in Minnesota and then as a madam.

The couple did not have children, but Isadore continued to support his mother. He was the Minneapolis contact for the New York mob boss Meyer Lansky, and Yiddy was a good friend of Lansky's as well. Like Lansky, Isadore and his brothers invested big money in Florida real estate, and Isadore also had more properties in Minnesota besides his own home at 3417 West Thirty-Eighth Street in Minneapolis. He owned the Dome Theater Lounge at 507 Hennepin Avenue, listed in the phone directory as "Minneapolis's newest and smartest night club—continuous entertainment."[211] The FBI suspected that he was still running the Flame, at 1605 Nicollet Avenue, as well as the Happy Hour Bar at 1523 Nicollet Avenue and sundry other businesses. In addition, Isadore "admitted that he and his crowd own a one-half interest in the El Cortez Hotel [in Las Vegas]."[212]

A 1945 FBI report on crime conditions in Minnesota mentioned that Isadore told the Bureau in 1942 that he was a U.S. citizen. The writer of the '45 report believed that this was an honest mistake, but Isadore said at another time that he learned he was not a citizen during the Liggett murder trial.[213]

The '45 report also noted that "Kid Cann has a great deal of persuasive power with the City Council in Minneapolis and is in a position to get practically anything done with the Council members that he desires."[214] However, Deputy Police Inspector Eugene Bernath told Mayor Humphrey's Law Enforcement Committee in August 1945 that there was no longer organized crime in Minneapolis. Bernath assured the committee that "all gambling houses have been closed although there may be sneak games operating that may run until I catch up with them."[215] Said the FBI report, "Mayor Humphrey further stated that they are moving in on the underworld, and there are members of the law enforcement agency, the police department, who are itching to show the underworld who's the boss around Minneapolis."[216] Humphrey would learn before too long who was the boss around Minneapolis.

Sir Galahad

Isadore's doctors saw signs of stress. In 1946, a duodenal ulcer plagued him. The flareups that would follow in later years were sometimes so bad that they brought "massive hemorrhages."[217] His health problems did not make him more cautious.

Around one o'clock in the morning on December 31, 1946, guests at the Nicollet Hotel were treated to unexpected free entertainment in the lobby. Isadore and three of his friends attacked a man named Rudolph Parapovich—and they lost. Parapovich trounced the four gangsters in front of onlookers. The police were called, and two squad cars arrived. They arrested Parapovich and drove Isadore to General Hospital, where he got stitches in his scalp. Isadore gave the pseudonym "J.B. Davis," but the truth came out before long. "'Kid Cann Gets Conked,'" reported the *Tribune*. "A hotel lobby fight in which Isadore 'Kid Cann' Blumenfeld, former bootlegger and underworld character, was badly beaten has kept night life devotees and loop characters buzzing for nearly two weeks, but [as of January 13] the Minneapolis police department has no complete official record of the incident." When reached for comment, Isadore said, "There is nothing to comment about, because I was not involved. I was not even in the city. I was in Miami Beach at the time." He said he had "heard about" the fight "even before I returned to Minneapolis." He claimed that he was "registered" in Miami Beach during that time, but when a reporter asked for the name of the hotel, Isadore said, "When I am in Miami Beach I stay with friends."

All the assailants denied involvement. Parapovich was fired from his job as a bouncer after the hotel fight (and fined ten dollars by the court for public intoxication).

Parapovich said that he entered the lobby and, seeing a girl from his hometown, Hibbing, he stopped to say hello. "Kid Cann…was…in a phone booth nearby. He seemed to become angry when he saw me talking to the girl because he yelled, 'Hold the wire, Chickie, here is some wise guy I've got to take care of.'…When Cann took a slug at me, I really went to work on him." The *Tribune* says, "From that point, accounts of the affair became less coherent"—because, of course, they did.

"Just what is this all about?" a *Tribune* reporter asked Chief of Police MacLean.

"It was just a fight."

"Did you know it was 'Kid Cann' who was beat up?"

"I was told who it was, unofficially, the next day."

"Did that information make any difference in your attitude when you discovered there was no report on what really took place?"

"No, I turned it over to [Detective Inspector Eugene] Bernath. After all there was no complaint and no prosecution."

"Isn't it customary for uniformed squads to make out a report of a serious fight in a leading hotel when prominently known characters are involved?"

"It is not necessary in the case of a little fight when no complaints are made."

"Well, in this case a man known about town was badly hurt. I should think that the police would have made an exception in such a case and reported immediately. Don't you think it might have led to more serious trouble?"

"No," said MacLean. "I didn't pay much attention to it, and I didn't know just what took place except that four men decided to beat up one man and got taken themselves."

"Then you wouldn't want to make an investigation of this?"

"No."[218]

The next day, January 14, Humphrey wrote a letter to Chief MacLean. He started, "Dear Mac" but crossed out "Mac" and handwrote "Chief." He said, "I have given considerable thought and study to the manner in which the police officers handled the case which involved Mr. Isadore

Blumenfeld....The officers involved...should be severely reprimanded for inefficient police work."

Humphrey, a former professor at Macalester College, slipped into lecture mode.

> *Minneapolis, like other major cities, has a few persons and characters who have repeatedly come under the observation of the Police Department because of their activities....Let it be a rule and principle of this administration that such persons as referred to above be given no special consideration by any member of our Police Department and that every officer clearly understand that it is his duty to apply the full force of the law upon such persons.*
>
> *The people of Minneapolis are sick and tired of having the good name of this city smeared by the activities and conduct of a handful of persons who have far too long had far too many privileges in this community.*[219]

Mayor Humphrey's response was reported in the *Tribune* the following morning. MacLean told a journalist, "No one would rather see Kid Cann behind bars than myself, but we must get some evidence of law-breaking to accomplish that." None of the witnesses to the fight had come forward with evidence, he said. "The lack of co-operation evinced by the public itself in giving evidence concerning characters and incidents centering around a public disturbance is amazing."[220]

Humphrey, who was out of town, had a telephone conversation with the chief on January 16, after which he wrote another letter.

> *I fully realize that you are completely loyal to me, and that you are following instructions as to the policy of our administration to be fair and equitable to all persons, whether they be in the public or in the Department. I know that your investigation has been detailed and is accurate....*
>
> *I have this request of you—there should be no more statements made concerning this incident. I think both of us recognize that it has already gone too far. I ask you to pass instructions...that the Police Department has no further comment....*
>
> *I want you to know, Mac, that newspapers are hungry for news and sometimes we get ourselves tripped up....*
>
> *It just seems to me, Mac, that when there is a case where someone has to take the blow, we at least ought to try to figure it out so as to spare the Mayor. I think you understand that. The purpose of my letter to you was*

> *because of the unfair and adverse manner in which the newspapers had handled the* [Kid] *Cann incident.*[221]

Humphrey let the press know that he considered the case closed. To him it was "like any other drunken brawl." All injured parties were having their bills paid by Abe Percansky of the Happy Hour Bar. "This is just some of this mystery that is inherent in the system of liquor around this town," said the befuddled mayor.[222]

Two days later, Bernath accidentally dispelled the mystery. At the Commonwealth Club, where he was expected to speak on the subject of "Veterans in the Postwar Police Department," he went way off script. In front of a crowd that included a district court judge, Bernath described Isadore as a "clean citizen." He only "wanted to be a Sir Galahad," and that night at the hotel, he "protected a woman who did not want protecting." Furthermore, Isadore ran a "clean place" at the Happy Hour. In the published report of his talk, Bernath was quoted as saying of Isadore that "as a citizen, he probably lives cleaner than most of us. He has to. He has a record." During the question-and-answer session, he said that the fight at the Nicollet Hotel was "just another drunken brawl with one drunk in it." He explained, "A drunk sees Kid Cann with a girl he knows from Hibbing. The drunk goes up to the girl, and says, 'Hello, hello old girl.' Kid Cann resents it, naturally. That started the trouble." Bernath would later deny saying that Isadore ran the Happy Hour. No consequences befell either him or Isadore.

George MacKinnon, among other critics of Humphrey, suspected the mayor (later senator and vice president of the United States) of accepting money from Isadore in exchange for letting Isadore operate in Minneapolis.[223] But although Humphrey, in his desperation for money, was lax about the source of his campaign funds, incontrovertible evidence of his knowingly bowing to Isadore's mob does not exist. If the mob had wanted Humphrey in power as badly as his detractors say it did, then his campaigns would not have repeatedly floundered as he was outspent by his opponents. Humphrey never would have accepted the vice presidency if he had had a ready source of cash that he could tap into for a future presidential campaign. A friend of his said later that four of Humphrey's close buddies advised him against being Lyndon B. Johnson's vice president. "We said [Humphrey would] lose his freedom. We said Johnson would cut his balls off." Humphrey had replied, "Look, I'm a poor man. I don't have rich friends….I just can't do it on my own. The only way I can become president is first to become vice president."[224]

If Isadore was willing to buy the allegiance of aldermen, surely he would have bought a presidential candidate—if that candidate had been open to bribery. Humphrey's colleagues in the Senate would reach the conclusion that he "always had money troubles and would take campaign contributions from anybody, giving little thought to where it came from. He was the kind of man who assumed that nobody he knew had bad motives."[225]

Besides money troubles, Humphrey had a habit of failing to stick to his guns. This would result in Johnson cutting off his balls in a metaphorical but spectacular fashion while Isadore's gang thrived for years to come.

An FBI report dated November 22, 1947, related that Isadore "was reported to have control of the horse racing wire service in Minneapolis. He also controlled the numbers racket in Minneapolis."[226] Back in 1945, investigative journalists had identified Minneapolis bookies as the "nerve center of the nation's betting on sports."[227] There was an obscene amount of money flowing through the gambling rackets in the city. Isadore, said the November 1947 report, also operated the Shipstead-Johnson Ice Show, and "Blumenfield was the principal racketeer in Minneapolis."[228]

An August 1949 FBI memo reported that "Kid Cann was operating a large gambling place at 1538 Nicollett [*sic*] Avenue, Minneapolis, where he had some $20,000 worth of fixtures and the place was run wide open."[229] Not long before that, a New York journalist was visiting Miami and had lunch at the Martinique Hotel with a friend. There were two men at another table, and the journalist's friend said that one of the men was named "Blumenfield," the pair of them "had most of the money in the Martinique" and the supposed owner was "more or less just a front."[230] The FBI received information that backed up what the journalist had heard. "Most of the interests in the Martinique Hotel [are] owned by Eddie Blumenfield [as he sometimes called himself], alias 'Kid Cann' of Minneapolis, Minn."[231]

An FBI report a year later cited a memo claiming that "Kid Cann, having made his pile, wants to go legit and settle in Miami."[232] His mother had died in 1948. Maybe that had sparked him to try. Maybe he did do his best from then on, but as a judge would later suggest, Isadore's sense of morality might not have been conventional.

In preparation for his move, "some of his Minneapolis holdings have been liquidated through Tommy Banks." The establishments he still owned included the Club Carnival, the Loring Liquor Store and the Flame. The memo added that a Minneapolis reporter went to one of Banks's saloons and asked the manager for further information about Isadore. The manager thought it was a shame the paper was digging into Isadore, "because the kid is just a good fellow who loans his money to a lot of friends." A day later, the manager told the reporter that he was invited to a convention in Miami, all expenses paid. A few days after that, a lackey of Banks or Isadore told the reporter that Isadore wanted to talk to him "because Cann has some plans that he don't want disrupted by a newspaper smear." And anyway, Banks's saloon manager said that Isadore didn't come to Minneapolis often. He just came to check on Harry and Yiddy and to collect money from debtors, whom the manager referred to as "those bums."

The same memo contained the colorful statement, "Cann also reputedly squires around a gal named Jean Hudson, a former model, Mrs. Cann doesn't like it a damned bit."[233]

It wasn't all fun and games for Isadore. After a falling out over a business arrangement, Isadore invited his former partner Eddie Holman to meet him at Club Carnival at 1523 Nicollet Avenue on July 28, 1949. There, Isadore attacked him, Holman defended himself and each man got a black eye.[234]

It is likely there were more fights than those that came to public notice, but people continued to do business with Isadore.

Chapter 6

THE RULE OF THE UNDERWORLD

Most Notorious Citizen

In a hideously dull address to the Kefauver Crime Committee (U.S. Senate Special Committee to Investigate Organized Crime in Interstate Commerce) on July 6, 1950, Governor Luther Youngdahl described Minnesota's war on slot machines. Things were going great, he said. He made a few bland recommendations to the committee, and they thanked him and praised him for being so willing to testify (not all state and local politicians were so forthcoming). Not once did Youngdahl mention Isadore.[235]

"Governor Youngdahl," said Senator Estes Kefauver, the chairman, "the committee is very grateful to you for appearing and giving us the benefit of your experience in the state of Minnesota. I know I speak for the committee in complimenting you and the officials of your State on a job well done."

"Thank you very much, Senator," said Youngdahl, "and I appreciate this opportunity."

"Mr. Peterson," said Kefauver, "will you come around, please? Mr. Peterson, I take it we can get started with your testimony."[236]

Virgil W. Peterson was the operating director of the Chicago Crime Commission. His testimony covered organized crime across the United States, including Minneapolis, where "a former candidate for mayor… claimed that he was approached by Kid Cann's group and offered a substantial contribution to his campaign fund. In return this group wanted to name the chief of police."[237]

Governor Luther Youngdahl as a young man in 1923. *Courtesy of Hennepin County Library.*

Daniel P. Sullivan, operating director of the Crime Commission of Greater Miami, had a good deal to tell the Kefauver committee about Isadore and friends' real estate deals. "In the Martinique Hotel in Miami Beach, Isadore Blumenfield…has been stated from a number of sources as being a large owner of that property.… We found that Blumenfeld, Berman, and… others either jointly or individually, or partially between them, owned [an incredible number of hotels, apartment buildings and lots].[238]

Investigators and the press closely followed Isadore's business activities, not only his real estate deals but also his ownership of stock in the Twin City Rapid Transit Company (TCRT).

Locals to this day blame Isadore for the destruction of the streetcars, but this is an unfair charge against the gangster. For one thing, he was but one of several malefactors; for another, the loss of the streetcars might have come with or without him.[239] There was a nationwide movement away from streetcars and toward buses and cars. Besides, the TCRT suffered from management problems, and its finances were in terrible shape by 1949. Charles Green, a New Yorker who characterized himself as "always ready to make a fast buck," invested in the TCRT.[240] Growing impatient with the realities and expenses of running a public transportation company, he looked for support in a plan to make it profitable for himself—which is to say wring it dry, Green being an early iteration of a vulture capitalist.

Green sought to gain control of the company, and he had an ally, Detroit lawyer Bigham D. Eblen. James B. Aune, an employee of the brokers through whom Green had purchased some of his TCRT stock, brought Green and Eblen to the Club Carnival and introduced them to the owner—Isadore. Aune, during the conversation that followed, brought up the fact that Isadore owned stock in the TCRT and made reference to Green's issue. In confidence, Green asked Isadore what he knew about Fred Ossanna, a local attorney whom Aune had suggested could help Green. Isadore "recommended Ossanna very highly. Green, much impressed by Kid Cann, decided Ossanna was their man."

Green hired Ossanna. They met often with Isadore at Club Carnival. Other investors ended up siding with Green, and he demanded that management resign, as he had "more than enough votes to oust them at the next stockholders' meeting." They resigned in November 1949, and Green and his allies got control of the TCRT. Green became president. Eblen was chairman of the board. Ossanna was legal counsel and then a director. Green raised fares, fired almost 25 percent of employees and cut schedules, "forcing thousands of citizens to freeze on street corners for long waits during Minnesota's harsh subzero winter." Then he discontinued the lines with the fewest riders, "a bitter blow to more thousands whose regular transportation between home and job was thus abruptly cut off." Green responded to the resulting outcry from riders, the press and public officials with, "The public be damned! I intend to force a profit out of this company! If necessary, I'll auction off all the streetcars and busses and sell the rails for scrap iron!" He threatened to cancel all service to St. Paul because "there was too little profit in it." The State Railroad and Warehouse Commission (SRWC) got a court order that restrained the TCRT from cutting more lines without a hearing.

Trolley cars, 1921. Streetcars were a feature of the cityscape for generations. *Courtesy of Hennepin County Library.*

Ossanna and Green quarreled over company policy. Eblen told Green that if he was looking to sell his shares and be done with the TCRT, Eblen knew some willing buyers back in Detroit who would take them off his hands. Green sold Eblen the shares to sell to his Detroit friends, but really, they were locals who were allies of Ossanna, and some of them were gangsters, including Isadore and Tommy Banks. Ossanna got control of the company in this way. He openly discussed schemes for bribery, one of which involved paying off aldermen.

That hardly sounds like Isadore's fault, but there was a firestorm over gangster control of the TCRT. A slew of investigations followed, conducted by the SRWC, the Ramsey County Grand Jury, the Federal Securities and Exchange Commission, the New York Stock Exchange, the ethics committee of the Hennepin County Bar Association and the Hennepin County Grand Jury.[241]

A flurry of news articles in the autumn of 1950 covered the investigations and drew attention to the fact that Isadore and Banks were among the TCRT's stockholders.[242]

One rainy night in November 1950, Robert Smith, a police reporter for the *Minneapolis Tribune*, went to the Nicollet Hotel to meet Isadore. Far from being an exciting opportunity, this was more nerve-wracking than anything else. Isadore had requested Smith in particular. Smith expected that Isadore would try to intimidate him. He was "young…and felt vulnerable."

Smith met Isadore in the lobby of the Nicollet. There were two bodyguards there but no one else. Smith "figured they had herded anyone who might have been there to other spaces. No one would overhear the conversation."

"Hey, Smith," said Isadore, "what's that sheet trying to do to me?"

"We're just reporting the news," Smith replied. He had heard scary stories about Isadore, but tonight he seemed calm.

"I got a family, you know," Isadore told him.

Smith "didn't know what to say to that. [He] knew he had a family."

"And when you print that stuff, they get upset."

Isadore told Smith about how he helped his community: family, friends and synagogue.[243] Isadore was generous to the Agudas Achim synagogue. He was appreciative of the fact that it welcomed him when other congregations did not, according to Minneapolis journalist Angelo Cohn.[244] Agudas Achim disbanded in 1950, and Isadore may have been feeling raw about this when he was talking to Smith.

Smith asked Isadore why he was addressing this to a young reporter like himself instead of to the editors.

MISSISSIPPI RIVER
BOOM ISLAND
St. Anthony Water Power Co.
Wd. I.
BROADWAY
MAIN
MARSHALL
UNIVERSITY
SECOND
FOURTH
FIFTH
SIXTH
SULLY
4½ ST.
RAMSEY
GRAND
CALIFORNIA
RIVER ST.
BREWERY ST.
CROSS ST.
OREGON ST.
PUBLIC WHARF
WATER
SIBLEY
UPPER BRIDGE
St. Anthony Mill Company
HUMBOLT PUB. SCH.
TRADERS ADD.
MARSHALL ADD.
BOTTINEAU'S SECOND ADD.
BOTTINEAU'S ADD.
GOLDSMITH'S ADDITION
ORTH'S ADD.
SUTTER'S ADD.
BORUP'S ADD.
TOWN OF ST. ANTHONY
EWING & CHUTES ADD.
HETCHMAN'S ADD.
ORTH & HETCHMAN'S ADD.
(VINE ST.)
(LAKE ST.)
(GROVE ST.)
(PRAIRIE ST.)
(BEAVER)
(ELK)
(MOOSE)
(FILLMORE)
(HOLLAND)
(PEMBINA)
(GENEVIEVE ST.)
(ST. MARTIN ST.)
(ST. PETER ST.)
(ST. ANTHONY ST.)
(ST. PAUL ST.)
(WOOD ST.)
(DANA ST.)
ROLLINS ST.
(TODD ST.)
18TH AVE.
17TH AVE. N.E.
16TH AVE. N.E.
15TH AVE.
14TH AVE. N.E.
13TH AVE.
12TH AVE. N.E.
11TH AVE.
10TH AVE.
9TH AVE.
8TH AVE.
7TH AVE.
6TH AVE.
5TH AVE.
4TH AVE.
3RD AVE.
Lot 1
Lot 2
Lot 3
Lot 4
Lot 8
M. Shultz
C. Schultz
John Orth Brewing Co.
A. Tramp
John Patterson
S. E. Reed
Abby L. Newell
PAPER MILL
SAW MILL

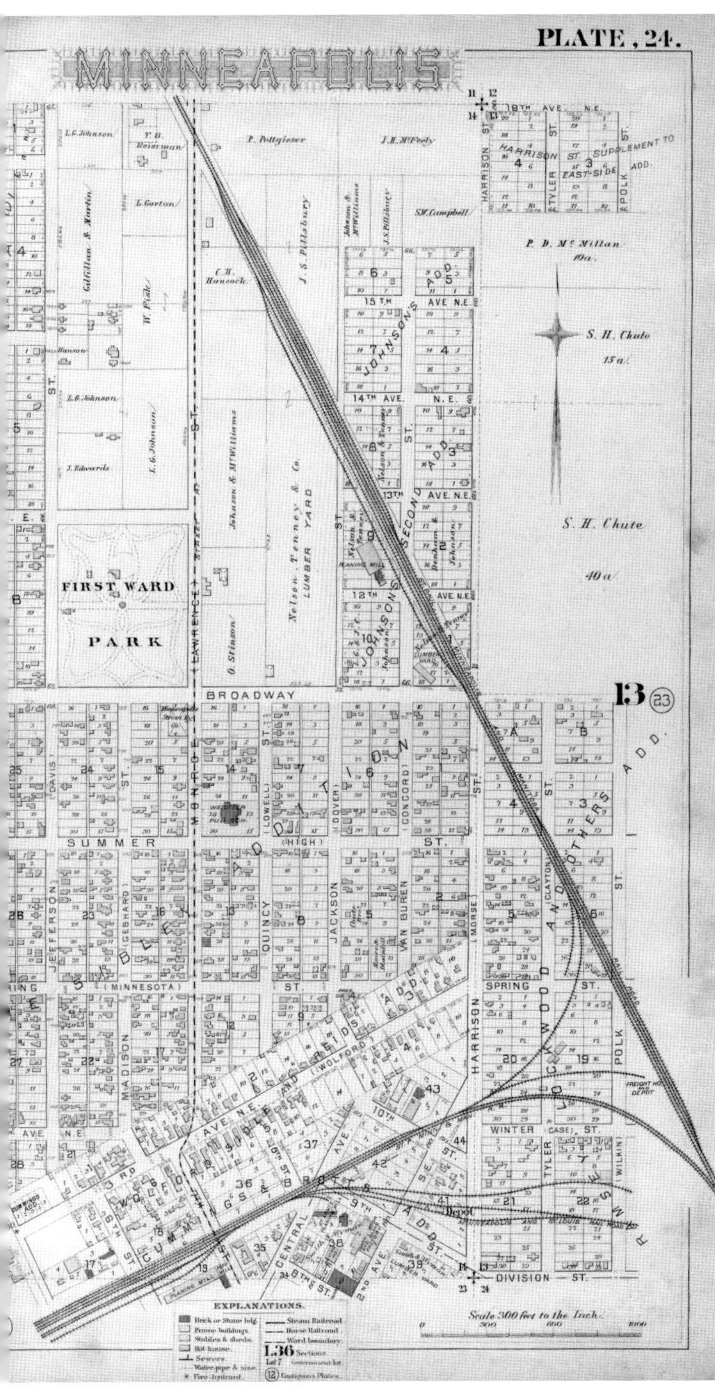

Map of Minneapolis, 1885. The "horse railroad" (the first streetcars) route is shown. *Courtesy of Hennepin County Library.*

Como-Harriet Streetcar Line. *Author's collection.*

"I don't know them," said Isadore. "You tell 'em."

It was still raining as Smith walked back to the office, where he told the editors what he had heard from Isadore. "Don't you start feeling sorry for him," one editor advised him.[245]

In September 1951, Gorden Schendel, a writer at *Collier's*, a magazine with national readership, reported on "How Mobsters Grabbed a City's Transit Line." In introducing Isadore to America, he was far meaner than the local journalists who had caused Isadore grief:

> *Isadore Blumenfeld, alias Kid Cann, alias "Dr. Ferguson," alias Fergie the Bull, is Minneapolis' most notorious citizen. Squat, swarthy Blumenfeld, or Kid Cann, not only is a gangster but looks it—from "sharp" tailoring to sinister stare. He has bossed the Minneapolis underworld—with…Tommy Banks—for 25 years.*[246]

By the time of Schendel's article, all the investigations into the TCRT had run aground. Ossanna was still in charge.

Kissing Off

On January 27, 1952, Eric Wingard reported in the *Tribune*, "Isadore Blumenfeld…says he is 'kissing off' Minneapolis as a place to live and will make his permanent residence in Miami, Fla." To this end, Isadore told Wingard, he was selling off his local real estate. "But all along Hennepin Avenue, there are expressions of doubt that 'Fergie' is removing himself from the Minneapolis scene," said Wingard. Isadore was too attached to his family and his friends in the local community, they said. "Blumenfeld always has exhibited a keen sense of loyalty" and was "devoted to his nephew and nieces."

Wingard asked Isadore about his first nickname, Kid Cann, and the fifty-one-year-old mobster grew angry. The name now represented, to him, a scapegoat for all crime in town. "It's persecution, and that's why I'm going." The negative press coverage about him "hurts them children" (referring to his siblings' kids). "Maybe," said Isadore, "if I leave town, people will let 'Kid Cann' die and my family can live in peace."

Isadore maintained that all his income came from legitimate investments: "stocks and bonds—like steel, Sears-Roebuck, Montgomery Ward and Seagram's Distilleries." He was annoyed by the scrutiny of his involvement with the TCRT. "My wife and I bought that stock as a favor to some people.…We got rid of every bit of it soon after we bought it—and we lost money on it."

Wingard noted that "some might consider the reputed multiple ownership of Minneapolis bar licenses as a 'racket' and the people involved as 'racketeers.'" Wingard explained to readers that sometimes "the 'front' borrows enough cash [from Isadore or his associates] to help fund the business, with the understanding that he can draw a certain amount each week as salary but must periodically split the profits with his backers." Isadore did admit to Wingard that he loaned money. "The greatest fellow that ever lived is the fellow who invented interest." But Isadore denied that this was a significant source of income for him. "I made my money bootlegging…and I've kept it by good investments like those I told you about." Wingard believed that, for all his money, Isadore's influence with the city council was waning.[247]

Isadore did spend an awful lot of time over the following decade in Florida, but as Wingard had predicted, he maintained a presence in Minneapolis. On December 11, ten and a half months after he kissed off Minneapolis, the *Tribune* reported that Isadore had been the victim of a burglary at his home, 5900 Oakland Avenue. This was noteworthy for two reasons. First, Captain of Detectives Bernath was once again in hot water: he was issued a warning by Chief of Police Thomas R. Jones for affixing a "no-publicity" notation to the police report (two officers were also reprimanded). Isadore had called Bernath at home about the burglary and told him that he didn't want publicity. The second reason for the break-in's noteworthiness is the items stolen, which included a diamond-set wristwatch worth $450; gold cufflinks with diamonds, worth $350; six dozen handkerchiefs that in total were worth $288; a dozen shirts that came out to $180; $250 worth of neckties; and $108 worth of underwear. That was just for Isadore. His wife lost, among other things, $70.80 worth of silk stockings, $363 of nightgowns and $150 of slips.[248]

Isadore's wealth and success continued to attract scrutiny. In February that year, a special Federal Rackets Grand Jury and the Immigration and Naturalization Service had begun investigating notorious characters, Isadore among them. Isadore's case was transferred to the St. Paul office to begin denaturalization proceedings, but they had to build a case against him.

On April 1 the following year, George E. MacKinnon was sworn in as U.S. attorney for the District of Minnesota. Afterward, an FBI agent told him that "Kid Cann was going up and down the alleys back of Hennepin Avenue and keeping track of the copper cable they were pulling out as they tore up the streetcar tracks on Hennepin." The agent did not know what this was about.[249]

The California Crime Commission's 1953 report described Isadore as an "ex-bootlegger who now as a millionaire shares the rule of the underworld."[250] That year, Isadore had one less person to share it with. Ed Morgan was found dead under horrific circumstances. His son, an attorney, got concerned when his parents didn't answer his phone calls and went to their Nicollet Avenue apartment. His mother's and father's bodies lay on the floor in the hall with a gun beside them. There was a suicide note from his father giving the reasons for this act: Morgan's eyesight was failing, and his wife had a chronic illness. Attorney Morgan's mother did not see it coming; she'd prepared a roast for the oven.[251]

Catharine Alice MacKinnon would one day create the legal argument for sexual harassment as sex discrimination in the United States and represent survivors of genocidal rape during the Bosnian War in a successful lawsuit against a Serbian official. But in the 1950s, she was a child, and her father, George, was the one fighting the legal battles. He would go down in local history as an antagonist to Kid Cann, whom he described to the Department of Justice as "the most notorious underworld character in this vicinity."

> *I was interested in Kid Cann and his tax problems, because his partner, Tommy Banks* [who had been convicted in 1952 of failure to pay income taxes] *complained about* [the authorities] *"going after him and not going after Kid Cann." I called the Internal Revenue and told them to begin looking at it. And I began looking at it in the grand jury.*[252]

In February 1955, the *Minneapolis Sunday Tribune* reported that the Hennepin County Grand Jury had conducted a "top secret" investigation to figure out why the IRS had not ordered a criminal prosecution regarding a $500,000 tax claim against Isadore. Theodore S. Anderson, the grand jury foreman, signed a report in which he recommended that the next grand jury continue to investigate Isadore "to determine if the income tax laws were properly applied."[253]

The next month, MacKinnon wrote to the Department of Justice with a basic explanation of the liquor store license issue.

> *Many of* [the people the grand jury investigated] *could not get liquor licenses in their own names for various reasons, including their generally adverse reputations in the community, prior convictions, etc. In a number of instances they accordingly operated by having the liquor store licensed in the name of a "front" man and the Bloom group, organized into varied partnerships, obtained excessive "rents" from these fronts."...In the instance of...one liquor store operated by* [a front], *the front was obligated to pay 10% of gross receipts as rent to* [Isadore] *and various partners.... Internal Revenue approved a settlement which we understand collapsed* [emphasis in original] *the operations of* [the front] *and* [Isadore and his associates'] *interests, and treated them as a partnership, and treated* [Isadore and his associates'] *interests as the actual operators of the business, a position they were not licensed to hold, and which they were ineligible to occupy under the local law.*

MacKinnon wished to "determine whether there was a conspiracy to evade and defeat the payment of income taxes." Isadore and his immediate circle had faced pressure from the IRS in the early '40s and had settled in and, at that time, reached an agreement with the Treasury Department by paying an amount that MacKinnon believed was based on misrepresentation of how they had handled their money. "That is an overt act [emphasis in original] which brings the entire conspiracy within the applicable statute of limitations."[254]

The Department of Justice replied that MacKinnon might or might not be correct, and it would be difficult "to establish that it was so clearly an improper settlement as to show criminal conduct on the part of those who negotiated it."[255] MacKinnon was not deterred in his mission to take on Isadore, even after a federal grand jury's 1957 investigation into whether Isadore had violated the Mann "White Slavery" Act ran aground. The Mann Act prohibited "interstate…transportation…for immoral purposes of women and girls," but the woman whom Isadore was believed to have "transported" for "immoral purposes" testified that he had done no such thing to her.[256]

The late 1950s were tumultuous for Isadore. It was during that period that Minneapolis Rabbi Albert Minda and his wife vacationed in Miami Beach. As they were sitting in the lobby of one of the hotels with which Isadore was associated, he walked over to them. He recognized Minda and "asked the Rabbi if he had time to listen to his life story." Minda "did not find time to listen."[257]

In January 1958, the federal grand jury subpoenaed records of Isadore's stock transactions. The jury was investigating reports of a $100,000 kickback from sales of scrap metal as the TCRT converted from streetcars to buses in 1953 and '54. MacKinnon was building a case against a slew of conspirators and was still working on the liquor license irregularities.[258] The FBI continued its own investigations, and so did the INS. The latter agency had chosen to pursue a case for moral turpitude, which would give them grounds to deport Isadore. They—and, subsequently, the FBI—learned that Isadore loved taboos. He participated in orgies and liked to watch socially unacceptable pairings, like White women with Black men. He also had mistresses.[259]

On May 5, 1958, Isadore "engaged in a violent argument" with Barney Berman in broad daylight at Grant Street and Nicollet, near the Loring Liquor Store. This appeared in an FBI report, along with notes indicating that investigators were keeping a close eye on developments with the Twin City Rapid Transit Company.[260] Isadore was well aware that he was being monitored, and it was weighing on him. In late June, one of his associates joked to an FBI agent, "I think you guys are the ones that caused him his ulcer."[261]

Shortly thereafter, as a pair of FBI agents were walking by the parking lot next to the Loring Liquor Store, Isadore "accidentally bumped into" them. The men had an informal chat, and Isadore told them that he had a bleeding ulcer. He had recently gone to the Mayo Clinic and had surgery to remove three-quarters of his stomach, and he would have to "take it easy for quite some time." He told the agents that "he cannot understand why the Federal authorities are putting him and his brothers to bed every night and also getting up with them in the morning." He insisted that neither he nor his associates were doing anything wrong, that they paid their taxes and that they "believe that someone has misinformed the Federal Government about their activities." When the topic of a highly publicized investigation into East Coast mobsters came up in conversation, Isadore

> *remarked that none of them are any good. He stated that they are very fortunate in Minneapolis not to have this type of underworld character. He stated that if anyone ever attempted to "muscle in" on them that they would certainly resist.*[262]

Ironically, what must have been the least stressful element of Isadore's life, sex, would be the start of his serious trouble. On September 1, 1958, the grand jury indicted him and Monte Perkins/Percansky, brother of Abe Percansky, on charges of transporting a woman across state lines for purposes of prostitution, in violation of the Mann Act.

Chapter 7

CAMPAIGN ISSUE

"I Know Nothing Kind About Him"

The following evening, September 2, at 6:40, MacKinnon, in the course of his campaign for governor, gave a speech on WCCO radio.

> *Tonight I am going to talk to you about…state liquor licensing laws in Minneapolis.…There is a group in Minneapolis who…have amassed great wealth by operating many liquor establishments in violation of the law. This group is known as the Kid Cann Liquor Syndicate.*

MacKinnon made it a political issue in his campaign, blaming DFL politicians for letting the Combination flourish unchecked.[263] In a radio address he gave one week later, MacKinnon pledged, "If I am elected governor I will [take action against Isadore's group]."[264]

There was no doubt that serious failures of leadership had occurred in Minneapolis, either from weakness, as in the case of Humphrey, or from corruption, as in the case of Marvin Kline and multiple city council members. The FBI believed that the Combination bribed Alderman George E. Johnson Jr., giving him a total of $12,000 between 1953 and 1956 (approximately $139,000 today).[265]

In October 1958, MacKinnon received an anonymous letter from a person who was very well-informed about Isadore's network.[266] "The city council was dominated all the time by Kid Cann," the writer alleged. A month after that, the mayor of Minneapolis requested that the Hennepin County Grand Jury investigate Isadore's liquor syndicate. In the same issue,

November 18, 1958, in which the *Minneapolis Star* carried the headline "Mayor Asks 14-Point Liquor Probe," it also reported that the grand jury was investigating the TCRT once more.[267]

MacKinnon railed in the press about Isadore's influence on politics. He accused the incumbent governor, Orville Freeman, of being "a rubber stamp for the Kid Cann liquor syndicate." Wallace Mitchell of the *Minneapolis Star* wrote up what he called a "lengthy interview" with MacKinnon. "The Kid Cann syndicate is right square in the middle of this campaign," said MacKinnon. Freeman's secretary told the *Star* that the governor had no comment aside from: "We still are waiting for MacKinnon to discuss the issues of the campaign."[268] MacKinnon lost the election. He was no longer U.S. attorney, either, just a lawyer in private practice, when the Hennepin County Grand Jury subpoenaed him to testify before it on December 22.

To MacKinnon's frustration, the next month, "the Hennepin County Grand Jury…whitewashed the entire operation of the syndicate without issuing a single subpoena for their books or records."[269] That same month, Isadore noticed blood in his urine. His doctors discovered that he had a bladder obstruction caused by his prostate. A minor medical procedure was required to fix the immediate problem, but the enlarged prostate would always be that way.[270]

On April 15, the *Minneapolis Tribune* reported, "Eight liquor firms under investigation by the Minneapolis police department for possible common ownership have submitted their financial records to the Minneapolis city council." As if anticipating police connivance on behalf of Isadore's syndicate, the mayor had ordered the MPD "to withhold any favorable recommendation on renewing the licenses until the books were submitted." The city council had only recently been granted the power to take this action. "The investigation followed charges by George MacKinnon, unsuccessful Republican candidate for governor, that the eight were controlled by a 'Kid Cann' liquor syndicate." However, "[a] grand jury found no violations of law in checking available evidence."

As for Isadore, "his house at 5900 Oakland Av. was reported for sale Tuesday," and rumor had it he was planning to move to Florida. "Blumenfeld has, however, on several occasions told newsmen he was moving permanently to Florida without doing so."[271]

But he was in Miami on September 22, 1959, when he surrendered to federal marshals so that he could be brought back to Minnesota to face charges of "fraud involving the Twin City Rapid Transit Co." and of violating the Mann Act.[272] On January 18, 1960, he pleaded not guilty to all charges.

Pretty Low

> *Throughout the preliminary legal bickering concerning the bond, Blumenfeld stood mute and motionless within a few feet of the judge....Showing evidence of the warm Florida sun on his swarthy face, Blumenfeld was dressed immaculately in a dark blue business suit, a white shirt with fancy gold cuff links, blue tie, blue stockings and polished black shoes.*[273]

Monte Perkins, charged with aiding and abetting Isadore in the Mann Act case, pleaded not guilty as well.

Blumenfeld's legal counsel filed a motion requesting a change of venue to outside Minnesota. On February 1, 1960, MacKinnon was called to testify about his public statements regarding Isadore. MacKinnon, uncharacteristically, hedged, and he downplayed his criticism during the campaign. But when defense attorney Thomas MacBride asked, "Did you ever say a kind word about [Isadore]?," MacKinnon replied, with his typical bluntness, "I know nothing kind about him."[274]

MacBride argued to the court,

> *One of the greatest reasons for removing a case from one jurisdiction to another is that there are powerful people in the particular jurisdiction the case is to be tried in who are against him and who have attempted to influence public opinion against him.*[275]

Judge Gunnar H. Nordbye denied the defense motion, remarking, "It would be a sad reflection on the caliber, stature, honesty and decency of the Minnesota citizenry if a jury of twelve impartial jurors could not be found among them."[276]

Four days after MacKinnon testified, Fallon Kelly, the current U.S. attorney, in company with three assistant U.S. attorneys and three special agents, spent the afternoon interviewing a beautiful young woman named Marilyn Tollefson. She had been Isadore's mistress in the mid-1950s, and in 1954, he brought her along with him when he drove around to watch streetcar tracks being pulled up and to inspect scrap piles and old streetcars at the TCRT car barns at University and Snelling Avenues. Afterward, they would eat at the Criterion restaurant on University.

Tollefson also told them that Isadore had mentioned to her by name the police officers "he could take care of," including Bernath. One of them was Russ Krueger, head of the Minneapolis Police Department Morals

Squad, who would later readily admit to the writer Christopher Valen that he had accepted small gifts and free drinks from Isadore's mob but did not feel beholden to them or afraid of them, raising the possibility that Isadore exaggerated his power to impress Tollefson. He "casually bragged [to her] that he could do almost anything through his connections with Minneapolis aldermen." The FBI had long known that Isadore had Alderman Henry Bank in his pocket—but Bank was no longer in office.

Tollefson revealed that Isadore played rigged games. Yiddy ran floating crap games in Minneapolis as well as in Shakopee, where he also ran a roulette wheel. And it "was common knowledge, she stated, that owners of a piece of a particular casino in Las Vegas would receive part of their cut through rigged winnings on the gambling tables."

Tollefson said Isadore had bombed one of his associates' homes. She said that when she and Isadore were in Chicago in the spring of 1958, they met the gangster Moe Dalitz, who "at that time wanted to kill Cann." She said, "Cann is very proud of the fact that Lil, his wife, does his laundry."

Isadore prostituted Tollefson to government officials, and "through his efforts she was prevailed upon to accommodate in her bedroom" a municipal court judge and a state supreme court justice, as well as the chief probation officer for Minneapolis, Ernest Meili, who "indicated to her that he would see that [one of Isadore's friends] got a break in exchange for her favors."[277]

At the trial, Tollefson said that she'd spoken to Isadore a few years earlier, when the federal grand jury investigated in 1957, and his "only comment was that they were getting pretty low when they were trying to indict him on his sex life." The reason, she said, that she eventually turned on Isadore and went to the FBI was that she was afraid he would kill her because he was angry that she kept asking for money.[278] She had been fond of Isadore when they were dating, and when her family disapproved, she chose Isadore over them. Back then, she said, she thought Isadore was "the finest man alive." He used to give her fifty or one hundred dollars each time they had sex.

In what must have been an uncomfortable moment in the courtroom, Isadore's wife was asked to stand so that Tollefson could identify her. Tollefson did recognize her, having seen her once on an elevator at Harry's Café in Minneapolis. Prosecuting attorney Segell also asked Tollefson if she knew Robert Ossanna, Fred's son. Yes, she said. She met Robert with Isadore at a bar in 1954. They all went to a hotel together, and she "was intimate with both men."[279]

During cross-examination, Tollefson said again that she had lied to the grand jury to protect Isadore. "I've lied all my life," she declared, "but

I'm telling the truth here in court." Tollefson proved herself to be a fierce witness. She "argued heatedly at times" with MacBride over his questions and "at other times broke into loud laughter in ridiculing his statements."

When asked about Isadore's many aliases, she said she had heard people refer to him as Kid Cann, but not to his face. They addressed him as Mr. Ferguson. But, she said, "I always called him Fergie—or papa."

Tollefson had a troubled past and had lived in a state home for girls in Sauk Center after running away from home in Minneapolis in 1945, when she was only thirteen years old. In 1948, she ran away for good and traveled the country with a group of magazine salespeople. She married one of them, but in 1952, she left him, and the other salespeople, in New Orleans. "She has not been divorced, to her knowledge," noted a reporter.

Tollefson testified that she met Isadore in November 1953. "Before I met Fergie I was a real dumb little kid; afterward, I was a real prostitute." After she broke up with Isadore, she started drinking heavily and brought herself to the brink of alcoholism. "But after five months in jail as a material witness, I feel great."[280]

The reason for that protective custody was that Tollefson was attacked on September 23, 1959, by three of Isadore's associates. They tortured her by burning her with cigarettes.[281]

The prosecution's charge against Monte Perkins was that he helped Tollefson and Isadore make travel arrangements across state lines and sent Tollefson money for that travel. Perkins admitted to knowing Tollefson. He testified to meeting her in early 1954 at the Gay 90s, where he worked as a floor manager. Tollefson told him to come to her room at the Mark Twain Hotel a few times. She asked Perkins for money, and he obliged because he held a "deep affection" for her.

The defense objected to ten potential witnesses for the prosecution, "most of whom were panderers and prostitutes," on the grounds that their testimony was "intended only to incite and inflame the jury against [Isadore]."

The *Minneapolis Star* told its readers what the prosecution couldn't present to the jurors, who were sequestered and would not see it in the newspapers: "This group of witnesses reportedly were prepared to testify to a series of 'sex parties' which Blumenfeld allegedly attended at Owasso Blvd. motel in rural Ramsey county in 1955 and 1956."[282]

After closing arguments, in which the prosecuting attorney described Tollefson as a "no-good girl" and MacBride declared that his client was "too intelligent to become embroiled in the situation outlined by Miss Tollefson," the jurors retired to deliberate.[283] By 10:35 the next morning, they had

The Gay 90s. *Author's collection.*

reached a verdict. Twenty minutes later, the defendants and their attorneys were assembled in the courtroom. "As word that a verdict had been reached spread throughout the federal courts building, employees in the building gathered in the courtroom," but there were no other spectators aside from journalists and Isadore's brothers.

The clerk of court read aloud the verdicts on four charges against each defendant. To the first charge against Isadore and Perkins, she read "not guilty."

"Blumenfeld, who had appeared ashen-faced," wrote a reporter for the *Minneapolis Star*, "sat up straighter in his chair and the color returned to his cheeks." But when the clerk got to the next charge, "her word 'guilty' seemed to strike Blumenfeld sharply. He sagged in his chair and took on a dejected look." On the two charges after that: not guilty. "But the damage had been done, apparently, as far as Blumenfeld and Perkins were concerned. They sat dejected in their chairs while the clerk read the…final verdict, which was 'guilty.'"[284]

Judge Nordbye set aside one of Perkins's not guilty verdicts. On March 21, he sentenced him to a year and a day in prison. He sentenced Isadore to two years in prison and fined him $2,500.

Some good news came for Isadore on April 12. The Hennepin County Grand Jury had decided not to formally investigate the "Kid Cann liquor syndicate." The foreman of the 1958 grand jury, before which MacKinnon had testified, recalled that "the expense of the investigation was borne by the taxpayers and was, in my opinion, a purely political move upon the part of… candidates to make a campaign issue at the time."[285]

Chapter 8

HOUNDING A MAN

Got Religion

Isadore still had to sit through the TCRT trial almost as soon as he was sentenced for the Mann Act violation. It was an awkward trial. Instead of a joint defense team, each of the six defendants on trial had his own attorney(s), "battling the government separately….[They] take turns cross-examining the government's witnesses." And Isadore "appears to be even more alone in the cast than the other defendants. His assigned place with his attorney…is a table in a corner…farthest from the jury box." Isadore didn't feel like socializing. "During the mid-morning and mid-afternoon court recesses, Blumenfeld usually stands alone in the fourth floor corridor," and he "seldom partakes of the coffee breaks arranged in an anteroom for prosecuting and defense attorneys and defendants." They didn't want to be associated with him, either. "Before the trial started the other defendants attempted to obtain trials separate from that of Blumenfeld."

Regardless,

> *Blumenfeld usually comes to court impeccably groomed and dressed in expensive but conservative dark silk and wool business suits, shoes, sox* [sic] *and ties to match. He has a weakness for alligator leather footwear. His thinning hair is sleeked back. He smiles easily. He exudes friendliness.*

For the first time in years, Isadore agreed to a newspaper interview. He told Larry Fitzmaurice of the *Minneapolis Star* that he had "made mistakes and done some wrong things" in his life. "Who hasn't?" Looking back at his prior criminal record and the last time before that year that he was in court, for the murder of Walter Liggett, he remarked, "That trial was an attempted 'frame.'" Isadore went on, "I've been rehabilitated for more than 25 years, but the authorities aren't satisfied with that. They keep hounding a man."

The evidence presented against him so far in the TCRT trial had established that Isadore was a stockholder, that he was in contact with Ossanna during the demolition of the streetcars and that he was on TCRT company property at the time of the conversion to buses. "I would like to know what's wrong with that," said Isadore. "Sure I was a stockbuyer. I had a lot of stock. Anybody with the money could buy it. It's sold every day on the New York Stock Exchange."

According to Fitzmaurice, "Every United States district attorney in Minnesota the last 20 years has attempted to nail Blumenfeld for income tax fraud....The returns of few taxpayers have been subjected to the repeated and constant scrutiny that Blumenfeld's have."

Isadore was almost sixty years old, and he told Fitzmaurice he had hoped that the rest of his life would be peaceful. "'And now this stuff comes up,' he added gloomily." He said that he spent much of his substantial income on charity. "I don't bar race, color or creed in giving money away." He donated to hospitals, religious organizations and charitable institutions. Both the Mann Act case and the TCRT case, to him, were "bum raps."[286]

Judge Nordbye must have agreed, at least in part, because on July 21, he granted a judgment of acquittal on three of the charges against Isadore, but nine remained.[287] A week later, Isadore's attorney, E. David Rosen, argued that his client was prosecuted because of his name, which had been sensationalized by reporters "so they could sell a five-cent newspaper."[288] Isadore was acquitted of the rest of the charges on August 6. Codefendants, including Ossanna, were convicted. Isadore barely got any breathing room. On October 8, the *Star* reported that the federal grand jury in St. Paul was expected to indict Isadore, Yiddy, Harry, Abe Brownstein, Barney Berman and some of their wives, in-laws and associates for violating the alcohol tax law. "The present federal grand jury probe is the result of more than 10 years of investigation of Blumenfeld's financial affairs by the federal government." This grand jury inquiry had been "stepped up" after the Hennepin County Grand Jury stopped its investigation.[289]

On October 21, the *Star* reported, "The federal grand jury in St. Paul reportedly returned a batch of indictments today aimed at crushing the so-called Kid Cann liquor syndicate which has flourished in Minneapolis since the prohibition era."[290] The jury believed that Isadore, Yiddy, Harry, Abe Brownstein and Barney Berman had "received more than a million dollars in three years from the profits of six liquor stores and bars licensed under other names."[291]

The defense moved for a change of venue to St. Paul, and Judge Edward J. Devitt granted it in December, explaining that he wanted the defendants to "feel sure they were getting an unbiased jury."[292]

MacBride had appealed Isadore's Mann Act conviction all the way to the U.S. Supreme Court, where it was turned down. Isadore had been freed on a $100,000 bond pending the appeal. He would soon have to surrender himself to serve his sentence.

In the current trial, Isadore, Harry, Yiddy, Berman and Abe Brownstein were all charged with "willfully and knowingly aiding, assisting, counseling and advising (the license holder [their front—there was a separate charge for each one]) in the preparation of a false and fraudulent (application) form 11 in which it was represented that (license holder) was the sole owner." The fronts, including Mrs. Brownstein, were charged with "fraudulently stating in the applications that they were the sole owners of the business places they represented."[293]

On March 2, one of the defendants was absent. She was excused for the time being because of a heart problem. Mrs. Brownstein was present but appeared unwell. Her husband and a codefendant had to help her to stand up. She asked to be excused for health issues also. Both women's trials would be postponed. Isadore "appeared to have aged since his last court appearance," wrote a reporter. "His then dark hair is now gray and the general appearance of good health he had then was not manifest yesterday in the courtroom."[294]

The defense argued that the defendants had acted in accordance with an agreement arranged with the Treasury Department in the early 1940s. Morris Grossman, an accountant who had been involved with the agreement, testified to this.[295] The defense did also stipulate a few days later that the defendants had "deliberately deceived Minneapolis city officials concerning the true ownership of several bars and liquor stores for nearly 20 years."[296]

Not long after that, Isadore told reporter Larry Fitzmaurice that he had "got religion," explaining, "I've done a lot of things in my life I'm not proud of and I'm trying to make amends." He said he had been "trying to go straight" ever since he got out of the workhouse after serving his sentence for violating the Prohibition Act. "He is a former president of a synagogue which disbanded several years ago," wrote Fitzmaurice. Historian Paul Maccabee says that he has never heard of Isadore serving as president, but "he was esteemed for his philanthropic giving to synagogues and was treated with respect during the High Holy Days."[297] Isadore was active in the affairs of his synagogue. According to Fitzmaurice, "At the time [of its disbandment], Blumenfeld said, he directed its assets be distributed equally among Jewish, Catholic and Protestant charities." Isadore also said he had "sought solace in the psalms." He told Fitzmaurice, "If I had not paid the government every dime I owe the past 25 years, you can be sure I'd have been prosecuted long ago. Instead, they dream up something nobody ever heard of."

The remaining eleven defendants, reported Fitzmaurice, "sit in rows of oak captain's chairs at the side of the courtroom like spectators of a drama. They display the outward detachment of persons with no interest in the outcome."[298] Isadore may have been detached because he felt assured of the outcome. He asked Monte Perkins to bribe a juror for him and gave him money for it. Monte Perkins was arrested ten days after Isadore told Fitzmaurice he'd "got religion."[299] Monte did not rat him out, though.

The bribery scheme was intercepted before the conspirators had made contact with the juror they were targeting. Because the jurors were sequestered in the Capri Hotel in St. Paul, the court was able to keep them in ignorance of this new development, out of concern that it might prejudice their verdict.

The next day, the *Star* reported, "Cann Liquor Syndicate Faces Disintegration." The Minneapolis City Council had finally, after decades of criticism on this point and under intense pressure from the mayor, refused to renew the Combination's liquor licenses, and six of their businesses were expected to be closed within the week. The INS served Isadore with a show cause order charging that "he is subject to deportation because of two convictions involving moral turpitude." Four of the codefendant "fronts"—Barney Berman's nephew, the sons-in-law of Isadore's sister Ethel and Isadore's own brother-in-law—were found not guilty. The other defendants whose trials had not been postponed were found guilty.[300]

"The defendants listened to the verdicts without emotion for the most part. The persons convicted by the jury stared at the courtroom floor or straight ahead." One of Ethel's sons-in-law "managed a brief smile at the recording of the verdict," and the other "dabbed at his face with a handkerchief."

Judge Devitt asked the convicted defendants if they thought it had been a fair trial, and they each said that it had.[301] Defense attorney Rosen tried to get his clients released on bail while they awaited the sentencing hearing. On account of the jury tampering attempt, Devitt ordered that the five syndicate members be held in the Ramsey County Jail until the hearing, but he released the two convicted fronts, Harry Bloom's sister-in-law Ruth Cook and Abe

Brownstein's sister-in-law Ann Albrecht, on $2,000 bail. Monte Perkins had an arraignment for bribery coming up the following week. He and Isadore were both headed to prison on Mann Act charges soon after that.

Judge Devitt assured the defense attorneys that he did not suspect them of involvement in the bribery attempt and told the federal probation department to conduct a presentence investigation. Each of the five syndicate members could receive up to twelve years in prison and a $20,000 fine; the two fronts could get nine years and a $15,000 fine.

Attendants at the Ramsey County Jail told the press that the convicts "were afflicted with sleeplessness their first night."

In early April, a rumor circulated among government officials that the federal grand jury would investigate Isadore for conspiring to tamper with the jury. Isadore went ahead and confessed. He told FBI agents that he had come up with the idea and provided Monte with the cash. And "I **NEVER** discussed this matter with other persons, including my co-defendants" (emphasis in original).[302]

Isadore's plea of guilty to conspiracy was entered. Al McConagha of the *Tribune* reported that "Blumenfeld appeared weary but composed. He made his pleas in a barely audible voice."

Devitt told Isadore to be "fully forthright" during the presentence process. Isadore said, "I certainly will. I absolutely will."[303]

Isadore certainly, absolutely was not. The probation officer remarked at one point in his report, "I do not believe defendant was telling me the truth but I was without any information of a tangible sort with which to draw out defendant in conversation."[304]

During the interview, Isadore

> *insists that he has not done a thing in his entire life which is really bad and that all of his present involvement was due to "politics." He wanted it understood that I would inform the Court that he is cooperating 100% in explaining his situation and that he was not being untruthful in any of his explanation. In no way does he wish it to appear that he has been guilty of any serious wrongdoing in* [the liquor stamp offense].

In regard to the bribery incident,

> *Defendant expressed in a very emotional manner that he was most sorry for his conduct in attempting to influence a juror or jurors. He considers that it has virtually destroyed his life's achievement and family reputation and he*

is "terribly sorry" that he did not then realize the seriousness of his actions as he does now.

On the subject of his prior record,

> *He claims that since his last conviction* [of violating the Prohibition Act] *and sentence to the Workhouse for a year he has never committed any offense for which he could be prosecuted, that is, except the matter of tampering with the jury as most recently happened. He held out his hands to me and asked me if I thought his hands were that of a killer or one who had ever used a gun on any other person. He stated that he had never held a gun on anyone nor had he ever owned a gun. I suggested that he did not have to do so but there were many under his influence who would do his bidding. I so stated to him on my first visit and discussion with him on April 11th. Apparently this accusation was quite disturbing to him because on April 17th he brought up the matter again and wanted me to be sure and understand that at no time in his life had he ever shot anybody or in any way harmed anybody. He stated that his life has been an honorable one except for his involvement in the bribery and that there was no organization as has been claimed and that he, as well as the other co-defendants, were "not bad fellows." As has been stated before, he states that because of politics during the past ten years he has been under scrutiny of many. He denies contributing to any political party or person running for public office. He denies associating himself with any syndicate of organized crime.*

There was an incident in Florida in which a man whom a witness thought was Isadore had pulled a gun on another man. When asked about it in the presentencing interview, Isadore said that he "did not recall" the occasion. He denied that he had blown up an associate's home.[305] He said that "he had never made a penny on bookmaking other than as a personal bet. He has never backed any book or participated in any book in any manner," and he said it was the same with his brothers. "In that connection he singled out Yiddy in particular, and said Yiddy is just a big boy at heart." If Yiddy had arranged for craps games to happen, said Isadore, it was "only because he was a good guy with respect to doing favors for friends who were getting married or for some similar event they had in mind."[306] Associates from outside the family contradicted all these points. "Both Yiddy and [Isadore] have been found at various bookmakers during raids conducted by the Intelligence Division."[307]

Isadore's wife was interviewed at their house on Oakland Avenue. She declined to criticize her husband. She appeared to somewhat blame herself for her husband's difficulties: "She is the homebody type and suggested that possibly the present situation…would not have come to pass if she had been more companionable and went with him wherever he did."[308] She visited him in jail morning and afternoon on visiting days, of which there were two per week.[309]

During his interview, Isadore was asked about his love affairs. He admitted to to having an affair with the gambler David Bohn's ex-wife and said he "has taken [a Las Vegas chorus girl] out a number of times."[310]

The probation officer assessed,

> *From observation and other sources of information it appears that defendant is of below average intelligence. He is an aggressive, ruthless individual and strong willed.…He thought that he should have a psychiatric examination primarily due to his, what he claims "stupidity" in attempting to bribe the jury."*[311]

Harry said in his interview that the bribery attempt "was the 'terriblest' thing that could ever happen and was suicide for him and the others for any defense which they might otherwise have had."[312]

Abe Brownstein "states that he is not alone in his opinion that Isadore's recent behavior is indicative of a degree of mental imbalance."[313] Yiddy agreed: "Isadore's recent actions and irresponsible comments indicate to [Yiddy] that he is mentally unstable."[314]

Even though the probation officers knew that Harry was "the financial advisor to the syndicate and also the principal director in financial matters," their presentence report on him was complimentary: "[Harry's] personal financial management bespeaks of integrity and sound policies.…[He is] most humble and contrite in his attitude."[315]

On the other hand, Isadore's report evinced disgust.

> *Defendant…has obviously built up an empire of individuals, both friends and relatives, with intentions of perpetuating it in succeeding generations. However, in so doing he has achieved nothing beyond material worth at the expense of others.*
>
> *Defendant has spoken of himself as being a salesman and this is more true than anything else that he can say. I suggest that he has not only been a salesman but a peddler of influence for many years. As long as I have*

> *been in the Probation Department I have observed that he has exercised his influence among law enforcement agencies in all levels of government. Today he has not outgrown this type of behavior. This is evidenced when he believed that he exercised influence when he sought to influence the jury by his intrepid behavior. The name of "Kid Cann" has been synonymous with gangsterism and ruthlessness for 35 years in this area and the community has in some respect condoned it and allowed it to flourish. He says that he is not a "bad guy." He has been a "nice guy" to many people who fell prey to his type of influence....*
>
> *Now that he has been caught in* [the liquor stamp] *offense which was motivated by greed and disregard of well-meaning government officials, he sought to circumvent the law boldly and without hesitation as in the bribery attempt. This was due primarily because he thought it was right so to do. His acquittal by the jury in the Twin City Rapid Transit case gave him further bolstering in his attitude that he was right. In that case it defies understanding how, because of his constant prominent appearances in all transactions, a jury would return a verdict as it did. Finally, defendant has spoiled lives of many people because of his corrupt attitude.*[316]

Isadore had not lost all that influence. Monte Perkins had been unwilling to give a statement to investigators in the bribery case until Isadore entered a guilty plea. He had feared for his family's safety. "You can never tell what could happen," he said. He had gotten threatening, anonymous phone calls.[317]

David Bohn was gloating, though. He told investigators that

> *Fergie Bloom has finally gotten his due and has been lucky all his life as he was in the transit case. He said Fergie bragged on the street for years during the TCRT conversion to the effect "Don't step on those rails, they're mine," "Watch the cable overhead, it's mine" etc. He said it was common knowledge among his friends that Fergie controlled the streetcar company during its conversion period, and masterminded the various frauds connected with it.*
>
> *He said he can't describe his feeling toward Fergie and his ex-wife, Dorothy. He said they are the lowest of people, have violated the various Ten Commandments, and he holds them in the greatest contempt.*[318]

Isadore was allowed to keep his pills for his heart condition in his possession in jail. His doctor said that his condition had worsened in the past year. Jailers told the press that Isadore "eats poorly and sleeps fitfully," but "despite his illness, Blumenfeld is a model prisoner."[319]

Not No Real Bad Man at All for Twenty-Five Years

"As the court well knows," said attorney Jones, at the May 18 sentencing hearing, "my client is quite limited in his ability to express himself and in this regard anything that the court may say in regard to the sanctity of our jury system is joined in by my client in the hopes that no other individual will violate this law." He did his best to make Isadore look sympathetic as he described his heart problems and his illiteracy—and besides, Jones said, he doesn't *look* like a criminal: "This man…does not resemble in any manner the two-gun snarling outlaw picture that has been painted of him.…There is a lot of good in this man."

"Mr. Rosen." Judge Devitt turned his attention to attorney E. David Rosen, who was cocounsel for Isadore and also counsel for the other four syndicate defendants (Charles T. Hvass was counsel for the women).

"Your Honor please," said Mr. Rosen, "not speaking as counsel for Mr. Blumenfeld in this matter, I should like to make this observation. When the news broke concerning the jury matter, quite frankly I was concerned about myself.…I was busy feeling sorry for myself." It took Rosen several days, he told the court, to "think about…why it came about…[and] I began to feel sorry for Mr. Blumenfeld."

That last statement is almost laughable, but Rosen's explanation was not: "I do not wish the court to…believe that I condone what he has done.…But…I do understand…that when I first met Mr. Blumenfeld in 1959…he was a sharp and perceptive thinker, had a quick mind and could respond." But over the past two years of their acquaintance, through his prior criminal trials, "I have watched this man deteriorate mentally. I don't think he is insane, your honor, but…he doesn't think clearly any longer."

Devitt asked Isadore's codefendants questions about their pasts, and then, finally, the moment came that anyone following the trial would have been most eager to hear. "Mr. Isadore Blumenfeld," said the judge, "do you have anything to say?"

> *Yes, sir, your honor. I realize that this is serious and all I can say is that I have destroyed myself, and I have destroyed my nephews, nieces and little ones coming up, and I am terribly, terribly sorry; and that's about all I can say, your honor.*

Devitt asked Isadore about his health problems, and Isadore gave a frank, clinical reply that ended with, "I've been just passing blood."

"I have been reading your whole record, Mr. Blumenfeld," said Devitt. "I don't know if you killed Walter Liggett or not."

"No, siree?" was Isadore's unsatisfying initial response. "They told me that before they arrested me even, I didn't but still they indicted me."

"I wasn't inquiring about it," the judge came back at him. "I don't know whether you killed him or not or these other people."

"No."

"I think the worst crime you committed was when you tried to bribe that juror."

"I imagine so," said Isadore.

"You know that is something that strikes at the very heart of America, just like a Communist, a spy—"

"I didn't realize that because—"

"Of all people, you should have been one to realize it, because you have been acquitted by juries so much in your life."

"Yes, sir. Yes, sir, I have."

"And this court bent over backwards to give you a fair trial."

"Yes, it did."

"But you weren't content with that."

"Well, I—"

"You wanted to make sure."

"No, I won't say that. It just got out of hand and it was really not meant that way at all….I have had so much trouble, your honor, for the past two and a half years that I am just fed up with it."

"Isn't that just an accumulation of troubles which you brought on yourself through the years?" the judge pressed him.

"No, I wouldn't say that," Isadore replied. "Maybe my earlier years, but I would say the past 25 years I think I have been well-behaved. I think I haven't been even active for the past ten years."

Devitt inquired incredulously, "Do you think your standard of ethics and morals and your dealings even in the past 25 years have been high or the same as other people or have you had your own standard of ethics?"

> *No. I would say I have been fair. I wouldn't do anything that's—I would say I wouldn't—if we thought we was violating this law or something like that, we sure didn't want no trouble and to the best of my knowledge what I thought is that we were told to do so and that's about the size of it. I haven't been no real bad man at all for 25 years.*

Judge Devitt questioned Isadore about other crimes he was suspected of committing and then commenced his preface to imposing sentence.

> *This case...has...shown a long-practiced scheme for willful violation... accompanied by open defiance of, and fraud upon, local police authorities—all for the great financial benefit of these defendants, and all to the moral debasement of the community....*
>
> *Their reputations are not good. The confessed effort of their leader to bribe the jury in this case was the most reprehensible act climaxing a long record of criminality. But over all has been spread an aura of righteousness and legitimacy characterized by an apparent (albeit in some cases, a genuine) interest in charitable and religious causes.*
>
> *These men were essentially bootleggers, and brought with them from the experiences of the prohibition era the disrespect for law and disdain for the integrity of public officials which characterized those times.*
>
> *Only the most naive would hesitate in suspecting that this long-time, extra-legal pursuit of substantial wealth was not accompanied by bribery of public officials. It is amazing that a large, intelligent community like Minneapolis could be visited for so long by the unhealthy criminal influence of an Isadore Blumenfeld and company.*[320]

Yiddy, Harry, Brownstein and Edward Berman were each sentenced to three years in prison and fined $20,000 "for aiding in the making of false statements in application for a federal liquor stamp." Five years of probation were to follow the prison term, on the condition that they did not "engage in any aspect of the liquor business." Ruth Cook and Ann Albrecht received two years' probation for "filing false statements of ownership of Minneapolis liquor establishments." Isadore received the same sentence as his brothers, Brownstein and Berman on the liquor stamp charges. But Devitt added on five years in prison and a $10,000 fine for "conspiracy to tamper with a juror."[321]

"You are not being treated bad at all," Devitt told Isadore.

"No, sir."

"For a man of your reputation. If it weren't for your sickness, illness, and you are 61 or 62?"

"61. Yes, sir."

"You will get good medical treatment in the hospital," Devitt assured him, as if Isadore did not already get the best doctors that money could buy. "I hope you do improve yourself there and read."

"That's what I'm going to do."

"You have led a bad life, Isadore. [Your attorney] doesn't want you to say anything, I guess, but you haven't led a very good life. You ought to think about that when you get over there."[322]

Chapter 9

"THE TWI-LIGHT OF MY LIFE"

Mercy, Not Justice?

June 15, 1961
Honorable Edward Devitt
Judge, United States District Court
Federal Building
St. Paul, Minn.

Honorable Sir:

I am availing myself of the privilege of addressing Your Honor, respectfully requesting, a Modification of the Sentence Your Honor imposed on May 16, 1961. As time is the [illegible] *of importance, due to the Law Authoring* [he likely meant "authorizing"] *Your Honor to entertain this Plea which is 60 Days from date of Sentence and with only 30 Days remaining, for Your Honor to act,* [illegible; possibly "know" or "humor"] *this appeal now, in the hope Your Honor, will allow Mercy, rather than Justice to Prevail.*

In the Twi-Light of my life, age 61, with a physical condition that is well known to Your Honor, I am hopeful Your Honor will be merciful.

I am at this time a Patient in the institution Hospital.

In Your Honor's deliberation, in reaching a determination, the very serious thought must occur to Your Honor, In view of the case. Should

I show, and extend to this man, the hand of Mercy. Should Your Honor, were I appearing now before Your Honor in person, ask now this question, I would in right, and good conscience reply, that I sincerely regret all that has occurred, and regret having caused so much trouble, to all concerned with this case.

I assure Your honor, I seek only Tranquility, for what yuse [sic] *it is God's will for me to live, I further assure Your Honor I seek only Peace and Happiness.*

I should like to Hope Your Honor will give Meticulous Study to my Plea for Modification of Sentence, making it possible, to return to my Home and Loved Ones.

For whatever consideration, Your Honor may Mercifully extend to me, be assured I will be most Grateful.

Hoping Your Honor, will act favorably on this appeal, and that I may have the privilege of receiving an acknowledgement of this letter. I am

With Profound Respect
Isadore Blumenfeld
78790. L.
U.S. Penitentiary
Leavenworth,
Kansas[323]

It does not appear that Devitt replied to Isadore's entreaty.

CONGRATULATIONS

Citation

Judge Edward J. Devitt:

In recognition of your courageous handling of the 1961 trials resulting in the curtailment of the activities of the notorious liquor syndicate in Minneapolis, we extend our most sincere congratulations and thanks!

We are also gratified by your conduct in matters which brought an awareness to the citizens for the need of a revitalized city government!

The Third Ward DFL Women's Club[324]

Dear Judge Devitt:

We are very thankful to you and the others that have brought an end to the Kid Cann syndicate.

Our heads are hung in shame that such an aggregation could continue in "a large, intelligent community like Minneapolis—for so long by the unhealthy influence of Isadore Blumenfeld and company."

Thank you again. Our confidence in due process of law has been renewed.

Sincerely,
G.T. Rugland[325]

Dear Sir:

I read the report in the paper last night of your sentencing and comments in the Kid Cann case. I felt very proud of you. I felt that what we know as American justice was finally catching up with a man whom I have known for many years and whose operations have always been either outside the law or just on the edge. It is inconceivable that a man with his experience would continue to operate that way, but apparently the wolf can't change colors.

It takes courage on the part of the Judge, and it takes the knowledge that he can't be reached politically to do what he did. I certainly want to commend you for your action.

Very truly yours,
Arthur G. Porter[326]

Dear Judge Devitt:—

Ever since reading your statement prior to sentencing the Syndicate members I have meant to write my congratulations on what, to me, was a real masterpiece and one which could not have been improved by adding or omitting a single word.

Mrs. Carlson and I spend several months traveling each year and Minneapolis' nasty reputation has been very humiliating to us....

Thank you for the pleasure I get from rereading the statement mentioned and showing it to my friends. I shall always keep it.

With kindest regards, I am

Sincerely,
Wilbur A. Carlson[327]

Devitt did not reply to all his fan mail—or if he did, some of the copies are lost. But presumably he found all of it gratifying.

VISITOR

Prison staff at Leavenworth were impressed with Isadore, who demonstrated "an exceptional ability to get along with his fellow inmate-workers," and he was recommended for a "meritorious service award."[328]

His burden was surely somewhat alleviated by the news that came on August 1, 1962, that the appellate court had acquitted him and all his codefendants of the liquor license charges. If only he had refrained from tampering and allowed the wheels of justice to turn on their own.

"Expressions of amazement and downright shock were heard from Minneapolis legal and official quarters," reported the *Minneapolis Daily*.[329]

MacKinnon was beside himself. On August 6, he wrote to Devitt,

Dear Ed:

The best local comment to date on [appellate judge] *Van Oosterhout is, "Where did he tend bar?"...*

I used to tell my assistants that one of the problems was to make a case so simple that the jury could understand it. They seem to have succeeded here in this respect but they did not make it simple enough so that the Court of Appeals could understand it....

> *This is a terrible decision...its judicial lawlessness....I find no support for the court's opinion except from Cann's lawyer....If the consequences were not so terrible, one could take something like this lightly, but it is decisions like this that do so much to discourage honest law enforcement.*
>
> *Best Regards,*
>
> *George E. MacKinnon*[330]

Isadore's parole date was set for September 16, 1964. His wife paid his fines, a total of $12,500: $10,000 for the bribery charge and $2,500 for the Mann Act charge. Officials at Springfield hospital prison, where Isadore had eventually been transferred on account of his poor health, said that he was a "cooperative prisoner."[331] Isadore was not deported after all. Romania may not have wanted him. A condition of his parole was that he no longer live in Minneapolis.[332] Isadore remained involved in organized crime, and he and his cohorts found themselves still surveilled by authorities, but now it was Florida authorities trying to build cases against them.[333]

Randall (not his real name), who was in his early twenties when he met Isadore after he got out of prison, remembers Isadore as "just such a sweet man. Polite....Fergie was funny." Randall also recalls that "when going out, Fergie drove a simple car" because "he was worried about" drawing attention to himself. But Randall describes him as "strong....He wasn't a wimpy guy."

Subtle signs of Isadore's power abounded in Miami Beach. One time, while vacationing there, Randall's parents went out to dinner with Isadore and one of his brothers. It was a popular restaurant, with a line snaking outside. The four of them didn't have a reservation, so they got in line. The manager walked over to them and said to Isadore, "Mr. Blumenfeld, your table is ready."[334]

Isadore was still permitted to travel to Minneapolis for temporary visits. In September 1965, he came back to attend Barney Berman's funeral. Isadore, Harry, Yiddy and Abe Brownstein were all pallbearers. "Blumenfeld, wearing a black suit, looked tanned and fit yesterday," reported Jim Parsons of the *Tribune*, "but acquaintances said that he has not been in good health."[335]

Financially, he was doing well. "Kid Cann Combine Is Top Miami Beach Landowner," reported the *Minneapolis Tribune* in 1967. Isadore now lived at the Executive House, an oceanfront apartment building. Yiddy was his neighbor.[336] Among the Combination's properties was the land under the famous Fontainebleau Hotel. "Indirectly," said a journalist, "a Minneapolis mobster gets a cut every time a tourist rents a $100 suite at the Fontainebleau."[337] The London *Daily Mail* took notice of them as well, reporting, "The Minneapolis group, anyone in the business will tell you, is a combine of rare and refined talents....They have become the warped symbols of local-lads-made-good."[338] The "group" shrank to Isadore and Yiddy. Harry lived a quiet life with his family in St. Louis Park. Abe Brownstein and his wife moved to the Southwest to care for their ailing son, Morris. He was only thirty-seven when he died in 1973, and his grieving father followed him three years later.[339]

In 1975, a reporter from the *Minneapolis Star* contacted Isadore in Miami Beach to ask for an interview, suggesting that it would show his "'human' side." Isadore retorted, "I've been a human a long, long, time, and I've been a damn good human."[340]

Isadore made an appearance in Minneapolis several times a year, and while there, he kept up a brave front. He told reporters Patrick Marx and Eric Pianin in December 1976 that he was "alive and well" and noted that he had outlived some of his "persecutors." Isadore instructed Marx and Pianin, "Tell 'em I'm looking good and feeling fine if you tell 'em anything." Maybe it was sour grapes, but he said, "I wouldn't come back to this city (to live) if you gave it to me" and described Marilyn Tollefson as a "two-dollar whore."

Among his "persecutors," he named three former U.S. attorneys, including MacKinnon, who were now judges and who had all worked on cases against him. "Blumenfeld maintains they got their promotions by making names for themselves prosecuting him."

A former alderman who had been an ally of Isadore's and had once been indicted in connection with the liquor license mess said that Isadore "was brave enough to stand up against the press....He was a tough cookie who wouldn't take the back seat to anybody. He wasn't as bad as he was pictured."

On his trips to Minneapolis, Isadore hung out in his stockbroker's office, smoking cigarettes and chatting with anyone who came by, all day long. "He sits here a lot and he's no different from anyone else except that he's up here a lot more than most," one stockbroker said. "Maybe years ago people would pay attention. But he's old now. He's no big deal."[341]

Around this time, Rhoda Lewin was conducting interviews with members of the local Jewish community. She wrote in her 1978 PhD thesis,

> *Blumenfeld paid a visit to Minneapolis while I was interviewing for this study, but a local newspaper reporter wrote a sensationalized feature on the visit and the Blumenfeld family and friends closed ranks and refused to talk to anyone else, including me.*[342]

She may have been referring to the Marx and Pianin article.

The predictably feisty MacKinnon drafted an angry letter to the editor of the *Minneapolis Star* that ran on for more than three typewritten pages and concluded with a demand that the paper launch its own investigation. "Then the public can determine whether [Isadore] was ever 'persecuted.' I suggest you proceed immediately to get this information."[343] He did not send that draft. In February, he sent a letter that said the same thing but more politely.[344]

On a visit home in June 1981, Isadore was admitted to Mount Sinai Hospital, where he died of heart disease on June 21.

Reminiscing about the chaotic times in Minneapolis post-Prohibition, Judge Devitt told a reporter, "Blumenfeld was part of the lore of those days. That was part of his lore—that he and his family and his gang dominated the criminal scene in Minneapolis."

Ed Ryan, who was now retired but had been Minneapolis chief of police and Hennepin County sheriff, maintained that the Humphrey administration "cleaned [the vice rackets] all out in 1945" and that was why Isadore "drifted away and went down to Miami Beach with his brother Yiddy." Ryan remembered Isadore as "soft-spoken....Those people are all salesmen. He dressed soberly. Those people were great at public relations because they had to sell themselves to the politicians, the public and especially the clergy, to keep everything quiet."[345]

Randall's mother told him not to come to the funeral because "they wanted to keep it small." Yet there were more than one hundred people at Isadore's burial service at Adath Jeshurun Cemetery, in spite of the heavy rain. Rabbi Max Shapiro of Temple Israel did not mention the name Kid Cann or any criminal activities or rumors thereof. "The cadence of the Kaddish," wrote reporter Bonnie Miller Rubin, "seemed even sadder when punctuated by the rain." Rabbi Shapiro gave a touching eulogy about Isadore's "generosity and his strong sense of family." He had never met the man, but he knew him by reputation, from people who loved him.

Mourners who spoke with reporters overflowed with anecdotes to back up Shapiro's assessment. "He was a wonderful fellow when a person needed something," said Harry Horowitz. "He helped out many a person who was broke." Rubin wrote afterward, "Many people recalled times when Kid Cann kept the wolf from their door, but no one wanted to be quoted by name."[346]

The journalist Eddie Schwartz said that Isadore "knew his way around and had a lot of friends, and he took care of his friends."[347] He knew Isadore to be a "well-mannered fellow," the type to "back away to live another day." He argued, "The prison records are all there and the court records are all there. He wasn't that bad a guy. He was a fairly easy man to know, he wasn't that difficult as people make him out to be as a brawler."

Abe Percansky agreed.

> *He was a very nice fella. What else can you say? What do you want to do, throw nails on top of his coffin? There was a lot of talk of him around town, all these stories. All those jealous people....He couldn't lick a fly, for Chrissake. The newspaper was the only one that made a gangster out of him. The man was a very generous, successful businessman. He was a generous character.*[348]

Isadore's crimes earned him a lot of money, which enabled his generosity, and all of it, the good and bad together, are why he became known as the "city's 'godfather.'"[349]

Epilogue

REMEMBRANCE AND REPRESENTATION

As I mentioned in the introduction to this book, sources of information on Isadore and his cohorts abound, some of them of dubious accuracy. But beyond the memories true and false, such as have been shared by those who knew him, and past the sometimes skewed information available in the "boxes full of old police files, judges' records, and microfilm of newspapers" found in the Minnesota Historical Society, lies Isadore's representation in a distinct collective memory, to which fiction gives voice.[350]

Isadore has multiple satire accounts on social media, posting in the voice of a rather vulgar Bugs Bunny. And that only scratches the surface of the fiction that his life has inspired.

In 1961, Gerald Vizenor, now an award-winning author and emeritus professor, was a twenty-six-year-old recent college graduate with an intense interest in an unsolved murder case. In his autobiography (first edition published in 1986, second edition 2009), he wrote,

> *I met with Minneapolis police officials to review the records of their investigation.... There was some resistance, some concern that my intentions were not personal but political; the police must be defensive about crimes they had never solved. A thin folder was recovered from the archives. The chief of detectives was surprised when he examined the file; he saw his name on a report and remembered that he was the first officer called to*

> *investigate the crime. He explained that he was a new police officer then and defended his trivial report. "We never spent much time on winos and derelicts in those days.... Who knows, one Indian vagrant kills another."*
>
> "[He] *is my father."*
>
> *"Maybe your father was a wino then,"* [the chief of detectives] *said, and looked to his watch. "Look, kid, that was a long time ago. Take it on the chin, you know what I mean?"*[351]

THE NEWS REPORTS ON his father's 1934 death could answer few questions. The *Minneapolis Tribune*, which one day would hire Gerald Vizenor on its writing staff, had this to say: "The slain youth was reported to have been mild tempered and not in the habit of picking fights. Police learned he had no debts, and, as far as they could ascertain, no enemies."[352] Clement Vizenor, an inoffensive housepainter, had died a brutal death, his throat cut so deeply that he was almost decapitated, his body left in the road like trash. There was no known reason for it. His son, who was a toddler when his father died, speculates that he "could have been a victim of organized crime."[353]

The Vizenor family's tragedy was compounded by the fact that Clement was their second loss in a matter of weeks. His brother, Truman, had died under what the *Minneapolis Journal* called "mysterious circumstances": he was "found in the Mississippi river...after he had fallen from a railroad bridge and struck his head."[354]

How does one make sense of such grief?

In Vizenor's 2010 book *Shrouds of White Earth*, an artist explains to a writer:

> *Clement always wore a fedora, and you look just like your father.... That was a horrible experience, your father and uncle murdered at about the same time, and the crimes have never been solved....*
>
> *Yes, you are right, the Minneapolis Truckers Strike was organized in the same year that we were born, 1934. I read that the brutality against strikers continued despite the resolution with the company owners. Gangsters were hired to menace union activists and communist supporters for several years after the strike. Your father and uncle were probably murdered because they were active in the union and truckers strike.*
>
> *Isadore Blumenfeld was the most notorious mobster at the time in Minneapolis. Kid Cann, as he was known on the streets...was a Jew born in Romania. This emigrant likely ordered the murder of your father and chased your fearful family back to the reservation. That was a time*

Band Box Diner. *Author's collection.*

> *of extreme emigrant irony. I read that he survived extreme prejudice and yet he became a gangster hired by companies in the city to threaten and murder natives, unionists, socialists, and communists. Kid Cann menaced any association with unions or communism.*
>
> *Really, he ate here, in this Band Box Diner?*[355]

Yes, Isadore really ate there, in the Band Box Diner, and according to local legend, he used it as a front.[356] But *Shrouds of White Earth* is a work of fiction. Vizenor returned to this story of the deaths of Clement and Truman Vizenor in 2020 with *Satie on the Seine: Letters to the Heirs of the Fur Trade*, an epistolary novel about Native puppeteers living and performing in Nazi-occupied Paris. A character visiting from the States tells them,

> *Clement and Truman were murdered in the same month.... The police never investigated the gangland crimes.... Clement and Truman were active in the union.... Most of our relatives were convinced that the boys had talked to federal agents about the time they refused to carry alcohol for the mobster Kid Cann from Canada through the White Earth Reservation to moonshine farmers in Stearns County during the Prohibition.*[357]

The true reason for the death of Clement Vizenor will never be found through available evidence, although the unprovable is not thereby untrue. How many are among the unacknowledged victims of Isadore and his Combination? It is a question without an answer.

CITY OF STONES, A police procedural novel by Christopher Valen and Dan Cohen, centers on the TCRT takeover and features major players in the Minneapolis rackets. Tommy Banks appears once, passively, as a cold fish, but Isadore Blumenfeld makes several appearances and exudes both warmth and menace. Valen and Cohen counted among their sources Russ Krueger, head of the Minneapolis Police Department Morals Squad. In the novel, Detective Cafferty, who passively accepted small gifts from the Combination while regarding it with frustration, serves almost as a metaphor for a city in flux, growing sick of its gangsters while it sees no way to unseat them.

In local attorney Todd M. Johnson's novel *Fatal Trust*, which takes place in 2018, the twenty-something protagonist gradually and painfully uncovers family secrets about his elders' connections to the Combination that shake him to his core, a process that some real-life people probably have experienced.

Italian singer/songwriter Paolo For Lee released a song in 2015 called "The Last Prayer (to Isadore Blumenfeld)."

In 2010, the Minnesota Landmarks and Lakeshore players performed a play about Isadore.[358] Mark Evans, Walter Liggett's grandson, wrote a screenplay about his father's murder, but it does not appear that it has yet been filmed.[359]

However, producer Michael Greenberg of North Coast Entertainment has been more successful, and his film *The Combination* was well received at the Trylon Cinema premiere. Isadore (played by local actor Ryan London Levin) is portrayed as a wild youth whose ambitions have begun to take form. Replacing the murder of the well-meaning Charles Goldberg with the fictional murder of an antisemite (played by Josh Cisewski), the film uses the concept of "Kid Cann as Jewish strongman" to explore lived reality for Jewish Minneapolitans in the 1920s.[360] The events leading to the shooting begin in a speakeasy that Harry and Isadore jointly own. They drink, smoke and flirt with women as they talk about their dreams for the future. The brothers are normal young people—aside from running a massive bootlegging operation. One of the women persuades Harry to dance with her, and a young man she rejected earlier in the scene attacks

Left: Official movie poster for *The Combination*. The Combination *Copyright North Coast Entertainment, LLC.*

Below: Isadore (*Ryan London Levin, left*) and Harry Bloom (*Luke Lebrun, right*) flirt with Ruth (*Gael Palen, second from left*) and Alice (*Emily Sue Bengtson, second from right*). The Combination *Copyright North Coast Entertainment, LLC.*

Isadore (*Ryan London Levin, center*) and Harry (*Luke Lebrun, right*) squaring off against Harry's assailant (*Josh Cisewski, left*). The Combination *Copyright North Coast Entertainment, LLC.*

the Blumenfelds, spouting antisemitic talking points. The other patrons at the speakeasy say nothing in the Blumenfelds' defense; a few express subtle agreement with the speaker. When the antisemite knocks down Harry with a hard blow, nobody comes to the latter's aid but Isadore, who beats the assailant and subdues him. Standing over their erstwhile attacker, Isadore tears into the crowd, challenging them to a fight. No one takes him up on the offer, and the man on the floor draws a gun. In the tussle for Isadore's life that follows, the gun goes off, and the man dies. Isadore has no regrets: "I'd do it again and again and again if I got the chance."[361]

While not a one-to-one capture of real life, this scene encapsulates the temptations and provocations that people in Isadore's position really did face. There is something morbidly fascinating in the local myth that the sinister figure "Kid Cann" corrupted nice, clean Minneapolis—and Minnesota state—politics. The reality is more complex, and more infuriating: Isadore was the antihero that Minneapolis deserved.

A GUIDE TO THE SOURCES

A Note About Collections

I relied heavily on collections for this project, a few of which require some explanation. The first is the Loren Hill Collection, assembled over many years by Loren Hill, a mob history enthusiast. It is at present a private collection, but Hill plans to donate it to an archive. He has accumulated thousands of documents on the Minneapolis and St. Paul mob and interviewed people who were socially connected to it.

The St. Paul Gangster History Research Collection (SPGHRC), housed in the Gale Library of the Minnesota Historical Society, was compiled by Paul Maccabee in preparation for his book *John Dillinger Slept Here*. "It's been picked clean," said Loren Hill glumly. I spoke to a librarian about pages that I found missing from an FBI file in one of the boxes, and she explained that, if anything were missing from the collection itself, then it would be noted in the file description. Another librarian mentioned to me separately that, because this is a popular collection, a lot of people access it, including school kids for research projects, and they don't always put things back in the same folders in which they found them. The SPGHRC materials can only be accessed while sitting at a table where the librarians can watch you using them, which lowers the risk of theft. However, there are pages in some documents that are disconnected from the first page or the original folder, so the context is not clear. Incidentally, this can be the case even for the less-accessed collections used in this project, because the politicians who donated—or whose heirs donated—their papers to the historical society often accumulated scraps of things like partial newspaper clippings or a page or two from the middle of a larger document that interested them. I have tried to be as specific as possible in my citations, but this is the reason for the occasional vagueness. All these collections are gold mines.

The bibliography includes the sources not fully cited in the endnotes, along with some uncited sources that were pertinent to the topic and that I used for background research.

List of Abbreviations in Endnotes

Blumenfeld, Isadore (Kid Cann). Minneapolis and Hennepin County Biography Files. Hennepin County Library Special Collections: BI

Edward J. Devitt Papers, Minnesota Historical Society: EJD

George E. MacKinnon Papers, Minnesota Historical Society: GEM

Hennepin County Library: HCL

Hennepin County Library Special Collections (for sources other than "BI"): HCLSC

Hubert H. Humphrey Papers, Minnesota Historical Society: HHH

Jews in Minnesota Oral History Project (oral history interviews), Minnesota Historical Society: JIM-OHP

Maccabee, Paul, St. Paul Gangster History Research Collection, Minnesota Historical Society: SPGHRC

Minneapolis Star: MS

Minneapolis Star Journal: MSJ

Minneapolis Tribune: MT

Minnesota Historical Society: MNHS

Minnesota Historical Society Press: MNHSP

St. Louis Park Historical Society: SLPHS

St. Paul Dispatch: SPD

St. Paul Pioneer Press: SPPP

Star Tribune: ST

University of Minnesota Press: UMP

Vince A. Day Papers, Minnesota Historical Society: VAD

NOTES

Introduction

1. Patrick Marx and Eric Pianin, "'Kid Cann' Outlived Many 'Persecutors,' Prefers a Quiet Life," MS, December 13, 1976.
2. Earl Wingard, "Kid Cann Says: I've Sold Out and Am Leaving Town," MT, January 27, 1952, BI.
3. Pre-Sentence Report—Isadore Blumenfield, April 21, 1961, EJD.
4. SLPHS, "Kid Cann and the Blumenfeld Family," https://slphistory.org.
5. MNHS, "Death Record: Blumenfield, Isadore," https://www.mnhs.org/search/people/death-records/d120db81-4986-4847-a41c-568b2e41cbf2.
6. Woodbury, *Stopping the Presses*, 190.
7. Wingard, "Kid Cann Says."
8. Lacey, *Little Man*.
9. "Kid Cann, Old-Time Crime Figure, Dies," MT, June 23, 1981.

Chapter 1

10. Curt Brown, "Two Days in Court, 25 Years Apart, Frame Minneapolis Mobster Kid Cann's Career," ST, August 7, 2021.
11. See, for example, E.J. Johnson, *They Call Me Kid Cann 1900–1980* (self-published, 1992), HCLSC, and Neal, *Augie's Secrets*.
12. Rivenes, *Dirty Doc Ames*, 12.
13. Lincoln Steffens, *Shame of the Cities* (Hill and Wang, 1957), 67–68.
14. Kristen Delegard, "Gentiles Only," The Historyapolis Project, March 6, 2015, https://www.historyapolis.com.

15. Laura E. Weber, "'Gentiles Preferred': Minneapolis Jews and Employment, 1920–1950," in *The North Star State: A Minnesota History Reader*, edited by Anne J. Aby (MNHSP, 2002), 393.
16. Wayne Wangstad, "'Kid Cann,' Onetime Underworld Figure in Minneapolis, Rites Held," SPPP, June 24, 1981.
17. Weber, "Gentiles Preferred."
18. Freedman, *Into the Bright Sunshine.*
19. Memorandum to the Files: Interview—Isadore Blumenfield, April 13, 1961, 6, EJD.
20. Pre-Sentence Report—Isadore Blumenfield, 13; "Alias Kid Cann," *Mpls.St.Paul Magazine*, November 1991, 88.
21. *Twin Citian*, "Kid Cann: A Myth or a Mobster?" June 1966.
22. Pre-Sentence Report—Yiddy Bloom, April 21, 1961, 5, EJD.
23. "Phillip Blumenfeld Addresses per Mpls Phone directories," SPGHRC.
24. FBI file MP 92-45, 8, LHC.
25. Pre-Sentence Report—Yiddy Bloom, 5.
26. Ernie Fliegel, interview by Rhoda G. Lewin, May 7, 1976, Jews in Minnesota Oral History Project, MNHS.
27. Howard A. Guilford, *A Tale of Two Cities: Memoirs of Sixteen Years Behind a Pencil* (self-published, 1929), 36.
28. Ibid., 48.
29. Maccabee, "Alias Kid Cann," 88–90.
30. See, for example, Berman, *Easy Street*, and Mayer, *The Political Career of Floyd B. Olson.*
31. Laura Weber, "From Exclusion to Integration: The Story of Jews in Minnesota," Mnopedia, last modified November 15, 2023.
32. Loring M. Staples, "The West Hotel and the Hostesses' Receptions and Balls," in *A History of Downtown Minneapolis and Saint Paul in the Words of the People Who Lived It* (Nodin Press, 1999), 103–09.
33. Kenney, *Twin Cities Album*, 123.
34. See, for discussion, Weber, "Gentiles Preferred."
35. Freedman, *Into the Bright Sunshine.*
36. Isadore Blumenfeld's Police Record, BI; Minnesota Statutes 1913, Section 8728, 8712, https://www.revisor.mn.gov/statutes/1913/cite/98/pdf.
37. Kristen Delegard, "The Measurements of Kid Cann," The Historyapolis Project, April 24, 2014, https://www.historyapolis.com.
38. Isadore Blumenfeld's Police Record, BI.

Chapter 2

39. U.S. Const. Amend. 18 (Repealed 1933).
40. United States Senate, "The Senate Overrides the President's Veto of the Volstead Act," https://www.senate.gov.

41. Joselit, *Our Gang*.
42. See Joselit, *Our Gang*, and Breines, *Tough Jews*.
43. Becky Little, "How Prohibition Fueled the Rise of the Ku Klux Klan," History.com, January 15, 2019, updated March 27, 2023, https://www.history.com.
44. Weber, "Gentiles Preferred," 383.
45. Lev Gringauz, "Jewish Mobster Kid Cann to Have Story Retold in Short Film Project," TC Jewfolk, October 31, 2023, https://tcjewfolk.com.
46. "Victim of Bank Bandit Is Dead: Chester Eklund Succumbs from Bullet Wound Inflicted January 20," MS, March 8, 1923.
47. Pre-Sentence Report—Isadore Blumenfield, 11.
48. Ibid., 12.
49. Office of County Attorney, Clay County, to Mabel Walker Willebrandt, Assistant Attorney General, Department of Justice, Washington, D.C., July 5, 1924, SPGHRC.
50. Brian P. Rubin, "The Forgotten Crime Boss," Citypages.com, April 22–28, 2015. Note: Citypages ceased publication at the end of October 2020. Archives are available at the Hennepin County Library and MNHS.
51. Isadore Blumenfeld's Police Record.
52. Twin Cities Music Highlights, "Cotton Club," https://twincitiesmusichighlights.net.
53. Goetting, *Joined at the Hip*, loc. 1901 (e-book).
54. Twin Cities Music Highlights, "Cotton Club"; Rubin, "Forgotten Crime Boss."
55. "Police Squads Hunt Gunmen in Twin Cities," MS, February 4, 1928; Twin Cities Music Highlights, "Cotton Club."
56. Police Officers Federation of Minneapolis, "James H. Trepanier," https://mpdfederation.com.
57. "Stanley Schiban," January 1, 1926, HCL Digital Collections, https://digitalcollections.hclib.org/digital/collection/MplsPhotos/id/79582/.
58. Rubin, "Forgotten Crime Boss."
59. Police Officers Federation of Minneapolis, "James H. Trepanier"; Rubin, "Forgotten Crime Boss."
60. "Cotton Club Battle Related by Patrolman," unidentified newspaper clipping, October 23, 1928, LHC.
61. Unidentified newspaper clipping, BI.
62. Police Officers Federation of Minneapolis, "James H. Trepanier."
63. Ibid.
64. "Cotton Club Battle."
65. Police Officers Federation of Minneapolis, "James H. Trepanier."
66. Unidentified newspaper clipping, BI.
67. Unidentified newspaper clipping, BI.
68. "Cotton Club Battle Related by Patrolman."
69. Police Officers Federation of Minneapolis, "James H. Trepanier."
70. Isadore Blumenfeld's Police Record.

71. South Dakota Public Broadcasting, "Verne Miller Time Line," https://sdpb.sd.gov/VerneMiller/timeline.asp; St. Louis Park Historical Society, "Kid Cann and the Blumenfeld Family," https://slphistory.org.
72. Rubin, "Forgotten Crime Boss."
73. South Dakota Public Broadcasting, "Verne Miller Time Line."
74. Federal Bureau of Investigation, File No. 63-385, Section No. 1, page 6 (citing Minneapolis file 62-1611-92), SPGHRC.
75. See, for example, Karlen, *Augie's Secrets*, 80 (e-book).
76. Guilford, *Tale of Two Cities*.
77. Mayer, *Political Career*.
78. MacGrath and Delmont, *Floyd Bjørnstjerne Olson*.
79. Brady, "Cold Blooded."
80. Mayer, *Political Career of Floyd B. Olson*.
81. See, for example, Harold Birkeland, *Floyd B. Olson in the First Kidnapping Murder in "Gangster Ridden Minnesota"* (self-published, 1934).
82. For a detailed explanation, see Johanneck, *Minneapolis Underworld*.
83. Pre-Sentence Report—Abe Brownstein, April 21, 1961, 2, EJD.
84. Robert D. Ford to Director of Prohibition, November 18, 1932, SPGHRC; "Pre-Sentence Report—Edward Berman," April 24, 1961, EJD.
85. Pre-Sentence Report—Edward Berman, April 21, 1961, 8, EJD.
86. SLPHS, "Tommy Banks."
87. Maccabee, "Alias Kid Cann," 90.
88. Pre-Sentence Report—Yiddy Bloom, 3.
89. SLPHS, "Tommy Banks," https://slphistory.org/bankstommybio.
90. Jewish Historical Society of the Upper Midwest, *North Side Memories*, 47.
91. Karpis and Trent, *Alvin Karpis Story*, 102–03.
92. Goetting, *Joined at the Hip*, loc. 307 (e-book).
93. Jewish Historical Society of the Upper Midwest, *North Side Memories*, 47.
94. FBI Minneapolis file 63-385, section 1 (citing 33-35-A-26, page 31), SPGHRC.
95. Fried, *Rise and Fall*, 104.

Chapter 3

96. Davis, *Minnesota 13*; Linda A. Cameron, "Agricultural Depression, 1920–1934," Mnopedia, https://www.mnopedia.org.
97. Davis, *Minnesota 13*.
98. Lewis L. Drill to G.A. Youngquist, October 26, 1932, 1, SPGHRC.
99. Ibid., 10.
100. Ibid., 5.
101. Ibid., 7–8.

102. Ibid., 13.
103. See: Alcohol Beverage Unit Supplemental Report, February 13, 1934, Case No. 2467—M, Case No. 2480—M, Bureau of Prohibition Files—Department of Justice, SPGHRC.
104. M.L. Harney and C.W. Hitsman to George F. Sullivan, Supplemental Report, Alcohol Beverage Unit Case No. 2467-M, Case No. 2480-M, February 13, 1934, SPGHRC.
105. Amy Lotsberg, "Drunk Chickens," 2021, *Volsteadland* (podcast), 56:04, https://redcircle.com.
106. Deanna Marie Huston, *The Hammonds of Lilydale: Life of Edward Delos Hammond and His Children* (Rosedog Press, 2020), 37.
107. Conversation with Sandra Brownstein, July 22, 2024.
108. R.E. Herrick, *Report on Bureau of Prohibition Case 236-S*, October 27, 1931, 424–25, SPGHRC.
109. Reid and Demaris, *Green Felt Jungle.*
110. R.E. Herrick, *Report*, 339.
111. Ibid. 372.
112. Ibid., 2–9.
113. Ibid., 131.
114. Ibid., 634.
115. Ibid., 637.
116. A.W.W. Woodcock, "Memorandum for Assistant Attorney General Keenan," June 13, 1934, SPGHRC.
117. Maccabee, *John Dillinger Slept Here*, 123–24 (e-book).
118. Harney and Hitsman, Supplemental Report, 30.
119. Larry O'Dell, "Urschel Kidnapping," Encyclopedia of Oklahoma History and Culture, https://www.okhistory.org; "'Davie the Jew' the Casinos King," *Odessa Journal*, February 13, 2021, https://odessa-journal.com.
120. Alcohol Beverage Unit Supplemental Report, February 13, 1934, Case No. 2467—M, Case No. 2480—M. 20, SPGHRC.
121. Ibid.
122. FBI file 63-385, section 1, serials 1–3, page 8 (citing 7-8-480, page 3), SPGHRC.
123. *U.S. v. Bates*, 77 F.3d 1101. 608-9, 1482.
124. Isadore Blumenfeld's Police Record.
125. True Bill, Case No. 10,478 in the District Court of the United States for the Western District of Oklahoma, August 23, 1933, 8.
126. J. Edgar Hoover, "Memorandum for the Assistant to the Attorney General, Mr. William Stanley," March 15, 1934, 2, SPGHRC.
127. MS, "Kidnap Suspects Fight Bail," August 26, 1933.
128. *U.S. v. Bates*, 77 F.3d 1101. 608–9, 1482.
129. Alcohol Beverage Unit Supplemental Report February 13, 1934, Case No. 2467—M, Case No. 2480—M. 18–19, SPGHRC.

130. *U.S. v. Bates*, 77 F.3d 1101. 608–9, 1482.
131. Ibid., 1303.
132. Office of the United States Attorney, District of Minnesota, to the Attorney General, March 29, 1934, 5, SPGHRC.

Chapter 4

133. M.L. Harney to George E. MacKinnon, May 2, 1956, 1, GEM.
134. "Trio Protest Innocence of 'Ride' Killing," SPD, December 21, 1933.
135. "Agents Seize Books of Racket Clique," SPPP, December 24, 1933.
136. "Althen Clue Sought in Liquor Ring Case," unidentified newspaper clipping, March 24, 1934, LHC.
137. "7 Plead Guilty in Rum Ring," MS, March 13, 1934.
138. Isadore Blumenfeld's Police Record.
139. John Phelan, "The Lesson of Prohibition," *Thinking Minnesota* no. 17 (Fall 2019): 26–30, https://www.americanexperiment.org.
140. Zac Farber, "Politics of the Past: When Minnesota Tried to Stop the Presses," *Minnesota Lawyer*, January 18, 2017, https://minnlawyer.com.
141. Kenney, *Twin Cities Album*, 150.
142. Ibid., 151.
143. Ibid., 155.
144. MacGrath and Delmont, *Floyd Bjørnstjerne Olson*; Mayer, *Political Career*; see also correspondence in the Vince A. Day Papers, especially the years 1931–35.
145. There are numerous excellent books on the strike. The most comprehensive among them is probably William Millikan's *Union Against Unions: The Minneapolis Citizens Alliance and Its Fight Against Organized Labor, 1903–1947* (Borealis Books, 2003).
146. This account is taken from Ellis's testimony for *The People of the State of New York v. Comprodaily Publishing Company, Inc., and Clarence Hathaway*, 262 *App. Dev.* 1008, 684–88.
147. Vince A. Day, letter to Walter W. Liggett, August 2, 1934, VAD.
148. Walter Liggett, letter to Vince A. Day, August 6, 1934, VAD.
149. See for example, Mitchell, letter to Walter Liggett, August 24, 1934, VAD.
150. FBI subject Edward "Barney" Berman, file no. 23-4687, section No. 1, serials 1–3, report October 8, 1935, 3, SPGHRC.
151. Quoted in Maccabee, "Alias Kid Cann," 91.
152. Hartman and Reusse, *Sid!*, 44.
153. Miller and Whereatt, "Rackets Figure Kid Cann, 80, Dies," MS, June 23, 1981.
154. Woodbury, *Stopping the Presses*, 79.
155. Ibid., 81.
156. Vince A. Day, "Memorandum for Governor," June 24, 1935, VAD.
157. Vince A. Day, "Memorandum," August 9, 1935, VAD.

158. Woodbury, *Stopping the Presses*, 85.
159. "Police Protect Kid Cann After Attack on Liggett," *Mid-West American*, October 30, 1935.
160. Woodbury, *Stopping the Presses*, 101.
161. Edith Liggett, letter to Roger Baldwin, SPGHRC.
162. Woodbury, *Stopping the Presses*, 119.
163. Woodbury, *Stopping the Presses*, loc. 1788–1815 (e-book).
164. Statement of Detective Higgins, December 12, 1935, Bureau of Criminal Apprehension Walter Liggett Murder File, SPGHRC.
165. Statement of Isadore Blumenfeld, December 9, 1935, Bureau of Criminal Apprehension Walter Liggett Murder File, SPGHRC.
166. Statement of Supervisor Hilborn, December 11, 1935, Bureau of Criminal Apprehension Walter Liggett Murder File, SPGHRC.
167. "Witness at Kid Cann Trial Is Discovered," MT, January 10, 1937, LHC.
168. Pre-Sentence Report—Isadore Blumenfield, 6.
169. Woodbury, *Stopping the Presses*.
170. Vince A. Day, "Memorandum to the Governor," February 10, 1936, 1–2, VAD.
171. George E. MacKinnon to Fred W. Friendly, July 22, 1980, GEM.
172. Ibid.
173. See, for example, Amy Lotsberg, "The Aftermath," 2021, *Volsteadland* (podcast), 32.24, https://redcircle.com/shows/volsteadland/ep/c74fb3bf-74a0-4c9f-8906-1a32905f21f3.
174. Writeup by Colston and Mealey, December 15, 1935; anonymous note; Bureau of Criminal Apprehension Walte Liggett Murder File, SPGHRC.
175. "Floyd B. Olson," August 26, 1936, *St. Paul Daily News*.
176. Jewish Historical Society of the Upper Midwest, *North Side Memories*.
177. C.W. Stein to Director of the FBI, November 25, 1936, SPGHRC.
178. "'Dreams' Laid to Kasherman," *Minneapolis Tribune*, January 15, 1937.
179. Berman, *Easy Street*, 134.
180. Benson, Michael, *Gangsters vs. Nazis*.
181. Berman, *Easy Street*.
182. Benson, *Gangsters vs. Nazis*.
183. Berman, *Easy Street*, 145.
184. FBI file 61-7587-194, 8, LHC.
185. Ibid., 143.
186. Unknown, St. Paul, MN, to Inspector [illegible], 4, FBI, June 19, 1939, re: FURDRESS (case information illegible), SPGHRC.
187. Ibid.
188. St. Paul FBI, Letter to Director, July 22, 1941, 3, SPGHRC.
189. "Mill City Publisher Slugged Fourth Time," SPPP, December 27, 1942.
190. FBI, Vice Conditions—Minneapolis and St. Paul, Minnesota, July 19, 1943, 6, SPGHRC.

191. Ibid., 23.
192. Ibid., 23–24.
193. Ibid., 24.
194. Ibid., 24, 31, 32.
195. January 21, 1942, quoted in Good Government League, *Soltau Condemned to Prison, Why?*, undated.
196. Selden Menefee, *Assignment: U.S.A.* (Reynal & Hitchcock, 1943), 101–02.
197. Hartman and Reusse, *Sid!*, 44.
198. Ibid., 42.
199. Ibid., 44.
200. *Excelsior Baking Co. v. United States*, 82 F. Supp. 423 (D. Minn. 1949).
201. Hynes, *Growing Seasons*, 277.
202. Ibid., 44.
203. Goetting, *Joined at the Hip*, loc 307 (e-book). See also, for example, Sherwin Linton, "I Don't Know If You've Got Enough Class to Make It in a Whiskey Joint," SherwinLinton.com, https://www.sherwinlinton.com.
204. *New York v. Comprodaily*, 262 *App. Dev*, 1008, 744–58.
205. January 3, 1940, EJD.
206. "Kline Administration Most Corrupt Regime in History of the City," *Public Press*, vol. 7.
207. "Kline Offers $500 Reward for Slayer of Kasherman," MSJ, January 23, 1945.

Chapter 5

208. FBI, *General Crime Survey Semi-Annual Report—St. Paul Field Division*, period from October 15, 1944, to April 15, 1945, SPGHRC.
209. Freedman, *Into the Bright Sunshine*.
210. Pre-Sentence Report—Isadore Blumenfield, 12.
211. FBI, *Crime Conditions—Minnesota*, 1945, 109, SPGHRC.
212. Ibid., 76.
213. Ibid., 76.
214. Ibid., 75.
215. Ibid., 195.
216. Ibid., 165.
217. Pre-Sentence Report—Isadore Blumenfield, 14.
218. MT.
219. HHH.
220. MT.
221. HHH.
222. "Mayor: 'Cann Case Closed,'" MT, January 14, 1947.
223. See files on Humphrey in the GEM Papers.
224. Carl Solberg, *Hubert Humphrey: A Biography* (Borealis Books, 1984), 240.

225. Ibid., 446.
226. FBI, Summary Memorandum, re: Isadore Blumenfild, June 8, 1955, EJD.
227. FBI, *Crime Conditions—Minnesota*, 22.
228. FBI, Summary Memorandum, re: Isadore Blumenfild, 3.
229. Ibid., 12.
230. Ibid., 2.
231. Ibid., 3.
232. Ibid., 10.
233. Ibid., 10–11.
234. MS, August 31, 1949.

Chapter 6

235. Investigation of Organized Crime in Interstate Commerce, *Hearings Before the Special Committee*, part 2 (U.S. Government Printing Office), 111–25.
236. Ibid., 125.
237. Ibid., 170–71.
238. Investigation of Organized Crime in Interstate Commerce, *Hearing Before the Special Committee*, part 1 (U.S. Government Printing Office), 164–65.
239. Eric Roper, "Was Organized Crime Behind the Demise of the Twin Cities Streetcar System?" ST, November 5, 2021. https://www2.startribune.com.
240. Schendel, "How Mobsters Grabbed Control of a TRANSIT Line," *Collier's*, September 1951, 72.
241. Ibid., 76.
242. See, for example, John Wickland and Earl Wingard, "Jury to Probe Green Charge That Ossanna Asked $20,000 to 'Buy' 6 or 8 City Aldermen," MT, November 3, 1950; Wickland and Wingard, "Kid Cann, Tommy Banks Face Call as Witnesses in Transit Firm Inquiry," MT, October 19, 1950.
243. Robert T. Smith, *Minneapolis Tribune*, June 24, 1981.
244. Angelo Cohn, interview by Rhoda G. Lewin, March 5, 1976, JIMOHP.
245. Robert T. Smith, *Minneapolis Tribune*, June 24, 1981.
246. Schendel, "How a Mob Grabbed," 30.
247. Wingard, "Kid Cann Says."
248. "Jones Probes 'Censorship' in Kid Cann Case," MT, December 11, 1942.
249. "Initiation of the TCRT Criminal Case," June 15, 1990, GEM.
250. Paul Nelson, "Blumenfeld, Isadore 'Kid Can' (1900–1981)," Mnopedia (Minnesota Historical Society), September 22, 2023, https://www.mnopedia.org.
251. "'Big Ed' Morgan, Wife Are Found Shot to Death," MSJ, July 14, 1953.
252. "Initiation of the TCRT Criminal Case," June 15, 1990, GEM Papers.
253. "Secret Probe of Kid Cann Case Revealed."
254. George E. MacKinnon to Department of Justice, March 22, 1955, GEM.

255. Department of Justice Enclosure 52751, September 21, 1955, GEM.
256. *Pub. L. 61-277*, https://uslaw.link/citation/us-law/public/61/277.
257. Lewin, *Some New Perspectives*, 282.
258. Larry Fitzmaurice, "Jury Subpoenas Brokers' Records," MS, January 30, 1958.
259. FBI file MP 92-45.
260. Ibid., 6.
261. SAC, Minneapolis to Director of FBI, June 27, 1958, Top Hoodlum Program Weekly Summary, LHC.
262. FBI SAC, Minneapolis to Director, FBI, July 11, 1958, LHC.

Chapter 7

263. Transcript of speech, GEM.
264. Transcript of speech, September 5, 1958, GEM.
265. Robert T. Smith, "The Decline and Fall of Kid Cann," MT, May 21, 1961.
266. Anonymous to MacKinnon, undated, Kid Cann—Miscellaneous folder, GEM.
267. Kid Cann—Miscellaneous folder, GEM.
268. Mitchell Wallace, "Kid Cann Is Issues, Says MacKinnon," MS, September 11, 1958.
269. MacKinnon, memo, 3, GEM.
270. Pre-Sentence Report—Isadore Blumenfield, 14.
271. "8 Liquor Firms Being Probed," MT.
272. Charles Hanna, "Kid Cann Surrenders to U.S. Marshal in Miami," MT, September 1959; Eric Roper, "Was Organized Crime Behind the Demise of the Twin Cities Streetcar System?" ST, November 5, 2021.
273. "Kid Cann Pleads Innocent on 22 Counts," MS, January 18, 1960.
274. Partial Transcript, Testimony of George Mac Kinnon [*sic*], *United States v. Isadore Blumenfield, et al.*, United States District Court, District of Minnesota, Fourth Division, February 1, 1960, 11. Note that "MacBride" is spelled "McBride" in some sources.
275. Ibid., 15.
276. "Kid Cann's White Slavery Trial," MT.
277. Memorandum to the File: Interview with Marilyn Tollefson, February 5, 1960, 1–8, EJD.
278. Al McConagha, "Blonde Says She Feared Kid Cann," MT, February 18, 1960.
279. "Once Liked Cann a Lot, Says Blonde," MS, February 17, 1960.
280. Phillips Shipley, "Defense Quizzes Miss Tollefson on Her Life 'Before Kid Cann,'" SPPP, February 18, 1960.
281. Pre-Sentence Report—Isadore Blumenfield, 8.
282. "Testimony Is Concluded in Cann, Perkins Trial," MS, February 20, 1960.
283. Al McConagha, "Cann Jury Studies Case for 4 Hours, Retires for Night," MT, February 23, 1960.
284. Al Woodruff, "Kid Cann, Perkins Are Found Guilty," MS, February 23, 1960.

285. "Grand Jury Won't Probe 'Syndicate,'" MS, April 13, 1960.

Chapter 8

286. Larry Fitzmaurice, "Bitter Blumenfeld Insists He's Been Good for 25 Years," MS, April 13, 1960.
287. "Kid Cann Cleared on 3 of 14 Counts in TCRT Trial," MT, July 22, 1960.
288. "Cann Called Victim of His Name by His Attorney," MT, July 28, 1960.
289. "U.S. Expected to Charge Kid Cann in Liquor Probe," MS, October 8, 1960.
290. "U.S. Indicts Cann & Liquor Associates," MS, October 21, 1960.
291. "9 Surrender on Liquor Charges," MT, October 22, 1960.
292. "Kid Cann Syndicate Trial Transferred to St. Paul," MT, December 20, 1960.
293. "9 Surrender on Liquor Charges," MT, October 22, 1960.
294. Al McConagha, "13 Accused of U.S. Liquor Law Violation," MT, March 2, 1961.
295. Al McConagha, "Kid Cann Accountant Says Syndicate Made Tax Agreement With U.S. in '41," MT, March 7, 1961.
296. Larry Fitzmaurice, "Mayor Says 'Cann' Licenses in Trouble." MS, March 8, 1961.
297. Paul Maccabee, communication with author, January 3, 2025."
298. Larry Fitzmaurice, "Blumenfeld Says He's Trying to Make Amends for His Past," MS, March 20, 1961.
299. Al McConagha, "FBI Arrests 2, Charges Attempt to Bribe in Kid Cann Liquor Trial," MT, March 30, 1961.
300. Larry Fitzmaurice, "Cann Liquor Syndicate Faces Disintegration," MS, March 31, 1961, LHC.
301. Al McConagha, "7 Convicted, 4 Acquitted in Liquor Syndicate Trial," MT, March 31, 1961.
302. Al McConagha, "Cann Admits Conspiring in Scheme to Bribe Juror," MT, April 6, 1961.
303. Larry Fitzmaurice, "Cann Pleads Guilty to Jury Bribe Try," MS, April 6, 1961.
304. Pre-Sentence Report—Isadore Blumenfield, 10.
305. Ibid., 1–10.
306. Memorandum to the Files: Interview—Isadore Blumenfeld, April 13, 1961, 4, EJD.
307. Bloom Group: Pre-Sentence Information, 6, EJD.
308. Pre-Sentence Report—Isadore Blumenfield, 12.
309. Memorandum to the Files: Interview—Isadore Blumenfeld, 11.
310. Ibid., 6–7.
311. Ibid., 14.
312. Pre-Sentence Report—Harry Bloom, April 21, 1961, 2, EJD.
313. Pre-Sentence Report—Abe Brownstein, 2.
314. Pre-Sentence Report—Yiddy Bloom, 5.
315. Pre-Sentence Report—Harry Bloom, 10.

316. Pre-Sentence Report—Isadore Blumenfield, 18.
317. Pre-Sentence Report—Monte Perkins, April 21, 1961, 11, EJD.
318. Memorandum of interview with David Bohn, re: Bloom Group, Minneapolis, April 11, 1961, 2, EJD.
319. "Blumenfeld Under Doctor's Care in Jail," MT, April 27, 1961.
320. "Here Is Partial Text of Comments at Cann Sentencing," MT, May 17, 1961.
321. McConagha, "Five Get Fines."
322. "Here Is Partial Text."

Chapter 9

323. EJD.
324. 3rd Ward DFL Women's Club, "Citation: Judge Edward J. Devitt," EJD.
325. EJD.
326. Ibid.
327. Ibid.
328. Maccabee, "Alias Kid Cann," 162.
329. "City Officials Shocked," *Minneapolis Daily*.
330. MacKinnon, letter to Edward J. Devitt, EJD.
331. "Kid Cann's Parole Date is September 16," MS, August 12, 1964.
332. Marx and Pianin, "'Kid Cann' Outlived."
333. See, for example, MT, "Florida Seeks to Close Hotels," October 20, 1969.
334. Conversation, July 27, 2024.
335. Jim Parsons, "Kid Cann Returns to Attend Funeral," MT, September 11, 1965.
336. Clarence Jones, "Kid Cann 'Combine' Is Top Miami Beach Landowner," MT, February 3, 1967.
337. Barbara Flanagan, MS, February 7, 1967.
338. Quoted in Al McConagha, "Kid Cann Group Intrigues Britons," MT, March 7, 1967.
339. Conversation with Sandra Brownstein, July 22, 2024.
340. MS, April 17, 1975.
341. Marx and Pianin, "'Kid Cann' Outlived."
342. Lewin, *Some New Perspectives*, 282.
343. See December 28, 1976 drafts of George E. MacKinnon to the Editor, *Minneapolis Star*, GEM.
344. George E. MacKinnon to the Editor, *Minneapolis Star*, February 8, 1977, GEM.
345. Wayne Wangstad, "'Kid Cann,' Onetime Underworld Figure in Minneapolis, Rites Held," unidentified newspaper clipping, LHC.
346. Bonnie Miller Rubin, "Mourners, Curious Follow Kid Cann to Graveside," MT, June 24, 1981.
347. Wangstad, "Kid Cann."

348. Kay Miller and Robert Whereatt, "Rackets Figure Kid Cann, 80, Dies," MS, June 23, 1981.
349. "City's 'Godfather' Comes Home to Die," MS, June 23, 1981.

Epilogue

350. Rubin, "Mourners, Curious Follow."
351. Vizenor, *Interior Landscapes*, 31–32 (e-book).
352. Quoted in Vizenor, *Interior Landscapes*, 29 (e-book).
353. Vizenor, *Interior Landscapes*, 28 (e-book).
354. *Minneapolis Journal*, June 30, 1936. Quoted in Vizenor, *Interior Landscapes*, 27 (e-book).
355. Vizenor, *Shrouds of White Earth*, 23–24 (e-book).
356. CBS Minnesota, "Guest Pass: Band Box Diner," https://www.cbsnews.com.
357. Vizenor, *Satie on the Seine*, loc. 1665 (e-book).
358. SLPHS, "Kid Cann."
359. Johanneck, *Minneapolis Underworld.*
360. Greenberg, interview by the author, June 24, 2024.
361. Greenberg, *Combination.*

SELECTED BIBLIOGRAPHY

Aby, Anne J., ed. *The North Star State: A Minnesota History Reader*. Minnesota Historical Society Press, 2002.

Benson, Michael. *Gangsters vs. Nazis: How Jewish Mobsters Battled Nazis in Wartime America.* Citadel Press, 2022.

Berman, Hyman, and Linda Mack Schloff. *Jews in Minnesota*. MNHSP, 2002.

Berman, Susan. *Easy Street: The True Story of a Mob Family.* Dial Press, 1981.

Breines, Paul. *Tough Jews: Political Fantasies and the Moral Dilemma of American Jewry.* Basic Books, 1990.

Brown, Curt. *Minnesota, 1918: When Flu, Fire, and War Ravaged the State*. Minnesota Historical Society, 2019.

Cohen, Rich. *Tough Jews: Fathers, Sons, and Gangster Dreams.* Vintage, 1999.

Davis, Elaine. *Minnesota 13: Stearns County's "Wet" Wild Prohibition Days.* 2007.

Downtown: A History of Downtown Minneapolis and Saint Paul in the Words of the People Who Lived It. Nodin Press, 1999.

Freedman, Samuel G. *Into the Bright Sunshine: Young Hubert Humphrey and the Fight for Civil Rights.* Oxford University Press, 2023.

Freshman, Phil, and Linda M. Schloff, eds. *North Side Memories: An Oral History of Minnesota's Largest Jewish Neighborhood.* Upper Midwest Jewish History, 2000.

Fried, Albert. *The Rise and Fall of the Jewish Gangster in America.* Columbia University Press, 1994.

Friendly, Fred W. *Minnesota Rag.* Random House, 2013.

Goetting, Jay. *Joined at the Hip: A History of Jazz in the Twin Cities*. Minnesota Historical Society Press, 2011.

Hartmann, John E. "The Minnesota Gag Law and the Fourteenth Amendment." *Minnesota History* 37, no. 4 (December 1960): 161–73.

Hartman, Sid, and Patrick Reusse. *Sid! The Sports Legends, the Inside Scoops, and the Close Personal Friends*. MVP Books, 2007.

Hynes, Samuel. *The Growing Seasons: An American Boyhood Before the War*. Viking Adult, 2003.

Johanneck, Elizabeth. *Minneapolis Underworld: Over a Century of Mill City Racketeering and Collusion*. Self-published, 2013.

Joselit, Jenna Weiffman. *Our Gang: Jewish Crime and the New York Jewish Community, 1900-1940*. Indiana University Press, 1983.

Karlen, Neal. *Augie's Secrets: The Minneapolis Mob and the King of the Hennepin Strip*. Minnesota Historical Society Press, 2013.

Karpis, Alvin, and Bill Trent. *The Alvin Karpis Story*. Coward, McCann & Geoghegan, 1971.

Kenney, Dave. *Twin Cities Album: A Visual History*. Minnesota Historical Society Press, 2005.

Lacey, Robert. *Little Man: Meyer Lansky and the Gangster Life*. Little, Brown, 1991.

Lait, Jack, and Lee Mortimer. *U.S.A. Confidential*. Crown, 1952.

Lewin. *Jewish Community of North Minneapolis*. Arcadia Publishing, 2001.

Lewin. *Some New Perspectives on the Jewish Immigrant Experience in Minneapolis: An Experiment in Oral History*. Doctoral dissertation, University of Minnesota, 1978.

Maccabee, Paul. *John Dillinger Slept Here: A Crooks' Tour of Crime and Corruption in St. Paul, 1920–1936*. Minnesota Historical Society Press, 1995.

MacGrath, John S., and James J. Delmont. *Floyd Bjørnstjerne, Olson Minnesota's Greatest Liberal Governor: A Memorial Volume*. Self-published. 1937.

Mayer, George H. *The Political Career of Floyd B. Olson*. University of Minnesota Press, 1951.

Menefee, Selden. *Assignment: U.S.A.* Reynal and Hitchcock, 1943.

Reid, Ed, and Ovid Demaris. *The Green Felt Jungle*. Pocket Books, 1964.

Rivenes, Erik. *Dirty Doc Ames and the Scandal That Shook Minneapolis*. Minnesota Historical Society Press, 2018.

Roberts, Rome. *The Minnesota Merry-Go-Round, or A Diary of the Legislature of the Age: The Best That Money Could Buy*. Minnesota Merry-Go-Round, 1935.

Rubenstein, Bruce. *Greed, Rage, and Love Gone Wrong: Murder in Minnesota*. University of Minnesota Press, 2006.

Salisbury, Harrison E. *A Journey for Our Times: A Memoir*. Harper & Row, 1983.

Shiffer, James Eli. *The King of Skid Row: John Bacich and the Twilight Years of Old Minneapolis*. University of Minnesota Press, 2016.

Vizenor, Gerald. *Interior Landscapes*. 2nd ed. SUNY Press, 2009.

———. *Satie on the Seine: Letters to the Heirs of the Fur Trade*. Wesleyan University Press, 2020.

———. *Shrouds of White Earth*. Excelsior Editions/SUNY Press, 2010.

Woodbury, Marda Liggett. *Stopping the Presses: The Murder of Walter W. Liggett*. University of Minnesota Press, 1998.

INDEX

A

B

C

D

F

G

H

J

K

L

M

N

O

P

R

S

T

V

W

Y

ABOUT THE AUTHOR

Ron has lived in Minnesota for nearly two decades. She went to Macalester College in St. Paul and the University of Minnesota Twin Cities for an MA in history and a PhD in sociology. She is also the author of *Minneapolis Murder & Mayhem* and *St. Paul Murder & Mayhem*. When she isn't reading and writing about history, Ron travels around the state with her family.